Texts *for* English Language
Development

BENCHMARK EDUCATION COMPANY

Table of Contents

Topic 1 • Government at Work

Essential Question

Why do we need a government?

The White House, Washington, D.C.

My Language Objectives

- Identify nouns
- Describe with adjectives
- Identify collective nouns
- Analyze prepositional phrases
- Write an informative/ explanatory essay
- Use past tense verbs
- Link ideas

My Content Objectives

- Build vocabulary related to government
- Understand the role of government and the jobs of people in government

2

police officers

soldiers

3

Smoke Jumpers

Smoke jumping was introduced in the 1930s by the U.S. Forest Service....

Smoke jumpers parachute from a plane. They land on a spot near the forest fire....

Smoke jumpers learn how to jump from a plane, handle a parachute, and land safely.

Once they are on the ground, they must be able to climb trees, use different saws, and work well in a team.

ThinkSpeakListen

Tell one key detail you learned about smoke jumpers.

Use Language: Nouns

plane

forest fire

parachute

team

Smoke jumpers wear special gear to keep them safe. Padded fireproof suits and helmets with face masks protect jumpers from fire, rocks, and trees.

ThinkSpeakListen

What nouns name the special gear smoke jumpers wear?

Can You Sew a Flag, Betsy Ross?

Mrs. Betsy Ross took a break from sewing to have tea and a biscuit. I sat on the floor nearby…

Then the door flew open. In walked General George Washington, the great leader of our army!…

"Our new country needs a flag," General Washington said…. "Can you sew a flag?…"

"I see that your stars have six points," Mrs. Ross said. "I think a five-pointed star would be better…."

⑤ The general agreed to the idea and left the shop. I watched as Mrs. Ross folded and cut long into the night.

⑥ For days, Mrs. Ross cut and stitched. Thirteen five-pointed stars and thirteen stripes represented the thirteen colonies.

⑦ When General Washington returned, Mrs. Ross proudly displayed the flag for him....

⑧ What a lucky mouse I was to be present on this important day in 1776!

ThinkSpeakListen

Summarize the story.

Our Flag

Our flag has thirteen stripes and fifty stars. The stripes stand for the thirteen colonies that first made our country. The stars stand for the fifty states we now have. Our flag has changed over the years. When a new state was added to our country, a star was added to the flag.

thirteen stripes
adjective   noun

fifty stars
adjective   noun

ThinkSpeakListen

Find one more sentence from "Our Flag" with a number adjective.

Use Language: Adjectives

Smoke Jumpers

Parachutes are another piece of **important** **equipment**.
                               adjective   noun

Their **bright** **colors** can be spotted quickly.
adjective   noun

Can You Sew a Flag, Betsy Ross?

In walked General George Washington, the **great** **leader** of our army!
                                             adjective   noun

"Our **new** **country** needs a flag," General Washington said.
adjective   noun

ThinkSpeakListen
Say the two words that are an adjective and noun in each sentence. What does the adjective describe about the noun?

Our Government's Laws by Kathy Furgang

A government is a group of people. The people work together to make important decisions for the country....

All governments make laws. A law is a rule that everyone has to follow....

Before 1984 no one had to wear a car seat belt. Then state governments began to pass seat belt laws.

Now every child in a car must wear a seat belt. That is the law. In most states, adults must wear seat belts too....

Laws help the government keep order.

Laws tell people what they can and cannot do....

There are laws about how fast a car can go.... There are laws about where a car can be parked....

Police officers work for the government....They all work to make sure people follow the laws....

ThinkSpeakListen

Explain what governments are and what governments do.

It is against the law for a car to pass a school bus that has stopped for students.

One day, a driver does not stop.... A police officer sees this.... The officer writes a ticket and gives it to the driver....

In a courtroom, a judge is in charge. The judge knows all about laws.

A jury is a group of people. They are chosen to listen to court cases.

ThinkSpeakListen

Explain what happens in a court. What do the judge and jury do?

Use Language: Collective Nouns

Collective Noun	Meaning
people	more than one person
police	more than one police officer
jury	the people who make up a jury
group	more than one of any thing

ThinkSpeakListen

Use each collective noun above in a sentence.

Class President: An Interview

Caleb: Rules? Rules are like laws. Kids might not like that! What new rules would you make?

Paula: My rules would solve problems. One rule I want is a longer recess. I also want music in the lunchroom....

Caleb: How will we learn about your new rules?

Paula: I am going to publish a list for the class to see.

Prepositional Phrase	Preposition	Noun
I also want music **in the lunchroom.**	**in**	**lunchroom**
Plus, it would be nice to have napkins **on the tables**.	**on**	**tables**
I am going to publish a list **for the class** to see.	**for**	**class**

ThinkSpeakListen

Explain what is happening in the photograph. Include a prepositional phrase. Use a preposition in the chart.

Write to Sources

Drawing on "Our Government's Laws," write a short essay that **explains** why it is important that a government makes laws. Use facts and details from the reading selection as the basis of your explanation.

Your topic

Purpose for writing

Source you will use

Sample Essay

Governments make laws to keep people safe.

There are laws about school buses and cars. A school bus may stop on a street. Children may get on or off the bus. When a bus stops to let children on or off, cars cannot pass the bus. The law says that cars behind the bus must stop. If cars move, children may get hurt.

The government made laws for drivers. The laws help keep everyone safe.

The first sentence tells the main idea.

The body presents details from the source. The details support the main idea of the essay. Laws about traffic appear in the source.

The conclusion reviews the main points of your essay. It also provides a closing statement.

15

Getting a Message to General Washington

by Susan Shafer

It was the afternoon of December 23, 1776.... Ben Franklin sat at his desk.... Franklin was talking about the Revolutionary War....

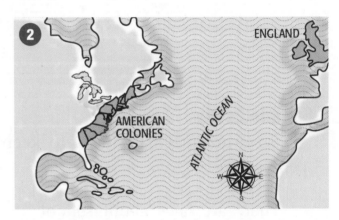

The colonies were ruled from far away in England.... So the people in the colonies declared war on England. They wanted to be free...

"Washington has a plan to defeat the British. But we don't know how we can get it to work," said Franklin....

Franklin explained, "See this map?... Washington wants to cross the river on Christmas and make a surprise attack...."

5

"Washington needs boats to cross the river!... I need to get him this message. The boats will arrive in two days...."

6

Then Tom had an idea. "Send me."...

7

Franklin looked at the eager boy.... "Here," he said... "Take this message to Washington. It is in a secret code." Off Tom went...

8

The British had found Franklin's secret message to Washington. "Bread. Cheese. Jam... What's this?" asked the soldier, puzzled.

ThinkSpeakListen

What problem does Tom help Benjamin Franklin solve?

"It's…just a list of food I need to get," answered Tom.…

Tom had fooled them! Only someone who knew the code could figure out that the words on the paper were about boats.…

"General Washington," said Tom. "I have an urgent letter from Mr. Franklin." Tom handed the general the paper.…

"Good work, young man," said Washington… "My men and I will be able to make our sneak attack on the British."

ThinkSpeakListen

How does Tom help solve the problem?

Use Language: Past Tense Verbs

Sentence	Present Tense Verb	Past Tense Verb
Franklin **looked** at the eager boy.	look	look**ed**
"Who are you?" **demanded** a soldier.	demand	demand**ed**
Tom had **fooled** them!	fool	fool**ed**
Tom **handed** the general the paper.	hand	hand**ed**

ThinkSpeakListen

Talk about the picture. Use past tense verbs in your sentences.

Here Comes the Mail

Sentence	Nouns	Linking Word
Police officers, teachers, and **mail carriers** are government workers.	Police officers teachers mail carriers	and
In **rain, snow,** or **hail**, mail carriers work.	rain snow hail	or

ThinkSpeakListen

Explain what mail carriers do. Use three nouns and a linking word.

Use Language: Irregular Past Tense Verbs

Sentence	Present Tense Verb	Irregular Past Tense Verb
It **was** the afternoon of December 23, 1776.	is	**was**
Ben Franklin **sat** at his desk.	sit	**sat**
The British had **found** Franklin's secret message to Washington.	find	**found**
Only someone who **knew** the code could figure out that the words on the paper **were** about boats.	know are	**knew** **were**

ThinkSpeakListen

Describe the picture above. Use a past tense verb from the chart.

What can we learn when we face problems?

My Language Objectives

- Use adjectives
- Analyze shades of meaning
- Use adverbs
- Use past tense verbs and adverbs
- Write an opinion essay

My Content Objectives

- Build vocabulary related to solving problems
- Understand how problems teach people lessons about life

23

Rough-Face Girl

Many moons ago, there lived a brave warrior. He was called the Invisible One.... He pledged to marry the first woman who could see him.

...There lived a man with two daughters. The elder daughter was callous and cruel but the younger, called Rough-Face Girl, was gentle and kind....

The Invisible One's sister greeted Rough-Face Girl. "Can you see my brother?... What is his bow made from?"...

"It's made from a rainbow!" Rough-Face Girl exclaimed. The Invisible One knew Rough-Face Girl could see him.

ThinkSpeakListen

Describe the characters in the story.

24

Use Language: Adjectives

Many <u>moons</u> ago, there lived a <u>brave</u> <u>warrior</u>.
   adjective noun

...There lived a man with <u>two</u> <u>daughters</u>.
      adjective noun

The <u>elder</u> <u>daughter</u> was <u>callous</u> and <u>cruel</u>.
  adjective   noun   adjective   adjective

The younger, called Rough-Face Girl, was gentle and kind.

ThinkSpeakListen

Describe one of the characters.

Yeh-Shen

1 Once upon a time, there was a girl named Yeh-Shen.... Yeh-Shen's only friend was a goldfish.

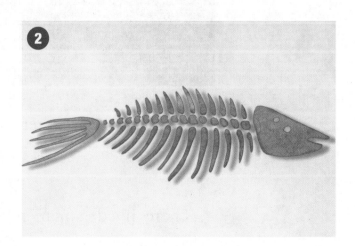

2 However, one day, her stepmother did the unkindest thing of all. She killed the fish and served him for supper.

3 As Yeh-Shen mourned...an old man suddenly appeared. "Gather the fish's bones," he said. "They have great power and can grant your wishes."

4 Soon it was time for the Spring Festival... Yeh-Shen wanted to attend. Alas, she had nothing but her plain, drab dress to wear.

5

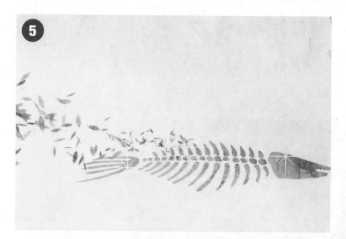

Yeh-Shen asked the bones for help. Her old dress and shoes disappeared immediately. In their place were a beautiful dress and golden slippers!

6

At the festival, Yeh-Shen was noticed by all, even the king! However, Yeh-Shen saw her stepsister staring at her, so she ran off quickly.

7

As she did, one of her slippers fell off.... One night, Yeh-Shen crept in. She grabbed the slipper and returned home....

8

When the king saw that the slipper fit her, he proposed. Naturally, they lived happily ever after.

ThinkSpeakListen
Summarize the story.

Willow and Toad

Long ago a princess named Willow <u>sat</u> at a well <u>and</u> <u>wept</u>.

                verb   link verb

"May I be your friend?" a toad asked as he jumped onto Willow's toe. "We can <u>sit</u> <u>and</u> <u>chat</u>!"

             verb link   verb

ThinkSpeakListen

Make up a sentence with two verbs. Link the verbs with "and."

Use Language: Linking Words

Rough-Face Girl

Idea	Linking Word	Idea
 The elder…was callous and cruel	but	the younger… was gentle and kind.

Yeh–Shen

Idea	Linking Word	Idea
 However, Yeh-Shen saw her stepsister staring at her,	so	she ran off quickly.
 She grabbed the slipper	and	returned home.

ThinkSpeakListen

Describe a scene from one of the stories. Use a linking word.

The Three Billy Goats Gruff

retold by Winston Ramos

Once upon a time there were three Billy Goats Gruff. There was a little Billy Goat Gruff....

There was a medium Billy Goat Gruff.... There was a great big Billy Goat Gruff....

The goats did not have enough to eat....

Over the bridge on another hill, the grass was green and sweet.

Under the bridge lived a bad-tempered troll. He would not let the goats cross the bridge....

One day the goats were so hungry they decided to cross the bridge....

"WHO'S THAT CROSSING OVER MY BRIDGE?" yelled Troll.

"Just me," said Little Billy Goat Gruff. "I am hungry...."

"Well, I am hungry, too," said Troll. "I'M GOING TO COME AND EAT YOU UP!" he roared.

"OH! Please don't eat me. I am little. Wait for my brother. Medium Billy Goat Gruff is much bigger," replied Little Billy Goat Gruff....

ThinkSpeakListen
Tell what the Troll does.

"WHO'S THAT CROSSING OVER MY BRIDGE?" shouted Troll....

"Please don't eat me.... Wait for my brother...."

"WHO'S THAT CROSSING OVER MY BRIDGE?" screamed Troll.

"You know it is me," called out Great Big Billy Goat Gruff....

Great Big Billy Goat Gruff stopped still. DOWN went his horns. He rushed at Troll....

"Ay!" cried Troll....
Great Big Billy Goat Gruff went *trip trap trip trap* over the bridge and up the hill.

ThinkSpeakListen
Tell what happens when Great Big Billy Goat Gruff sees Troll.

Use Language: Shades of Meaning

Sentence	Word	Shade of Meaning
"WHO'S THAT CROSSING OVER MY BRIDGE?" he <u>yelled</u>.	<u>yelled</u>	said loudly
"WHO'S THAT CROSSING OVER MY BRIDGE?" he <u>shouted</u>.	<u>shouted</u>	said very loudly
"WHO'S THAT CROSSING OVER MY BRIDGE?" he <u>roared</u>.	<u>roared</u>	a dull, deep cry, like that of a lion
"WHO'S THAT CROSSING OVER MY BRIDGE?" <u>screamed</u> Troll.	<u>screamed</u>	gave a long, loud, high-pitched cry

ThinkSpeakListen

Act out what Troll says and does.

Jack and the Bean Tree

Sentence	Present Tense Verb	Irregular Past Tense Verb
Jack <u>made</u> the trade.	make	made
Mother <u>did</u> not speak to Jack when he <u>came</u> home.	do come	did came
Jack <u>began</u> to climb it.	begin	began
At the top, he <u>saw</u> the feet of a mean giant.	see	saw

ThinkSpeakListen

Tell what Jack did. Use one of the irregular past tense verbs.

Use Language: Adverbs

The goats did not <u>have</u> <u>enough</u> to eat.

verb   adverb

Great Big Billy Goat Gruff <u>stopped</u> <u>still</u>.

verb   adverb

<u>DOWN</u> <u>went</u> his horns.

adverb   verb

Great Big Billy Goat Gruff <u>went</u>
<u>*trip trap trip trap*</u>....

verb

adverb

ThinkSpeakListen

Retell a part of the story. Use an adverb in your retelling.

35

The Troll Returns:
A Sequel to "The Three Billy Goats Gruff"

by Jeffrey Fuerst

Once upon a time, a mean Troll guarded a bridge over a river.

"Stay away!" Troll roared whenever anyone came near the bridge....

Then Troll saw an ad for Politeness School.... "Come to Politeness School. Learn to be nice."...

Politeness School was hard work.... Troll was the best student in the class!... Troll was now nice....

Troll did not get mad. He said, "Hello, goats.... Do not run. I am not mean anymore."...

5

Great Big Billy Goat Gruff looked at the smiling Troll....

"Oh, yes. I am. And thank you for noticing," said Troll.

6

"Well, since you are nice, I have a job for you. You can be the greeter at the bridge."...

"I would like that job!" said Troll. And he did—at first....

7

I am nice to goats, Troll thought. *I am polite. Not once has a goat said "Have a nice day" to me....*

8

"That is it!" yelled Troll....

"If you can't be polite and say hello, get off my bridge!"...

ThinkSpeakListen

Compare Troll from before Politeness School to Troll from after Politeness School.

9

Calmly, Troll said, "Being nice is not for me. It goes against my Trollness.... I will leave quietly."

10

"Wait," said Great Big Billy Goat Gruff. "We were wrong not to say 'thank you' to you. Let me make it up to you."

11

"I think I have a better job for you.... Your new job is to keep billy goats away from the water. We are not good swimmers."

12

From that day forward, Troll roared, "Stay away! Keep out!"...
Then, after the goat moved away, he added, "Have a nice day."

ThinkSpeakListen

What does Great Big Billy Goat Gruff do to help Troll?

Use Language: Past Tense Verbs and Adverbs

Sentence	The adverb describes *when* about the verb	The adverb describes *where* about the verb	The adverb describes *how* about the verb
I <u>am</u> not mean <u>anymore</u>. verb · adverb	✓		
And he <u>did</u>—<u>at first</u>…. verb · adverb	✓		
I will <u>leave</u> <u>quietly</u>. verb · adverb			✓
<u>Stay</u> <u>away</u>! verb · adverb		✓	
<u>Keep</u> <u>out</u>! verb · adverb		✓	

ThinkSpeakListen
What does each adverb describe about the verb: *when*, *where*, or *how*?

Why Sun and Moon Live in the Sky

Once upon a time, Sun had a home on Earth. Moon was his wife. They had a good life by the edge of the sea. Each day, Sun brightly woke up and took a stroll near the shore. At night, Moon sat under a palm tree and counted seashells.

One day, Sea came up to Sun and Moon with a seaweed pie. Sun and Moon were glad to welcome Sea, who was usually very shy.

Adjective	+ly	Adverb
bright	ly	brightly
usual	ly	usually
glad	ly	gladly
shy	ly	shyly

ThinkSpeakListen

Tell what happens in the story. Use an adverb.

Write to Sources

After reading "The Troll Returns: A Sequel to 'The Three Billy Goats Gruff,'" why do you think the goats were not polite to Troll? In a short essay, **state your opinion** and provide one or more reasons to support it. Use evidence from the text to support your opinion and reasons.

Type of writing

Purpose for writing

Source you will use

Sample Essay

The goats forgot that it is important to be nice to others.

The Troll was nice and let the goats cross the bridge. The goats were happy that they could cross. The goats also were hungry. They wanted to eat the grass on the other side. So the goats were only thinking about themselves. They forgot to show good manners. They could have said to Troll, "Thank you" or "Have a nice day."

The goats did not show good manners when they crossed the bridge. They forgot that being nice to others is important.

The first sentence states the opinion.

The body presents reasons. The reasons support the opinion of the essay. The text provides evidence to support the opinion and reasons.

The conclusion reviews the main points of your essay. It provides a closing sentence.

How do living things get what they need to survive?

My Language Objectives

- Use prepositional phrases
- Use proper nouns
- Analyze shades of meaning
- Use linking words
- Write to sources

My Content Objectives

- Build vocabulary related to plants and animals in different habitats around the world
- Compare and contrast habitats around the world

desert

coral reef

wetlands

43

The Coldest Place on Earth

Only a few tough animals can survive Antarctica's harsh winters. One of them is an amazing bird. Meet the emperor penguin!…

All the penguins waddle across the ice when it's time to lay eggs. Each mother lays one egg and then waddles back to the sea to eat.…

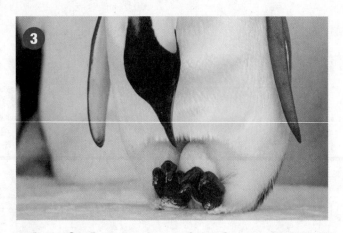

The fathers wiggle the eggs onto their feet, right under their bellies.…

Then one day, *tap, tap, crack!* The eggs hatch.… Soon the penguin families will return to the sea again.

ThinkSpeakListen

Retell a key detail.

Use Language: Prepositional Phrases

Prepositional Phrase	Preposition	Noun or Pronoun
One **of them** is an amazing bird.	**of**	them
All the penguins waddle **across the ice** when it's time to lay eggs.	**across**	ice
Each mother lays one egg and then waddles back **to the sea** to eat.	**to**	sea
The fathers wiggle the eggs **onto their feet**, right **under their bellies**.	**onto**	feet
	under	bellies

These penguins spend most of their lives in the freezing-cold sea. A thick layer of blubber, or fat, and shiny feathers act like a heavy waterproof jacket.

ThinkSpeakListen

Describe what penguins do. Use at least one preposition.

Postcards from Alex

"Are you sure you want to leave the rain forest?" asked Juan....

"It's always damp from the rain and too warm!" said Alex.

"But we have delicious insects here!" cried Juan.

"I'll find tasty bugs to eat elsewhere," Alex said. "And I'll send postcards to let you know where I am."...

Dear Juan,
I am in Chile.

A llama named Larry gave me a ride up a mountain. There's grass for me to burrow in, and the bugs are tasty....

Larry's fur coat keeps him warm, but I'm freezing. This is not a good home for me. I'm leaving!

*Your chilly pal,
Alex....*

5

Dear Juan,

Here I am in the city!

A mouse named Miguel showed me his favorite places to eat. He likes garbage, but I've found some fleas and spiders.

6

The problem is there's nowhere for me to sleep, because I can't dig a burrow. Even my big claws can't break these sidewalks. Good-bye city!…

7

Dear Juan,

I swam across a river yesterday.

Now I'm back on land in the desert. It's so hot and dry, I can't find a drop of water.

8

There isn't even an ant to eat.

The rain forest is best for me! I'm coming home!

Alex

ThinkSpeakListen

Retell the events that happen in this tale.

The Deserts of Utah

How does a plant live in the desert? The cactus might be the most unusual desert plant. It has sharp needles on it. They keep animals away. The cactus stores water in its stems and roots. The roots are only a few inches below ground. This helps the cactus get the water it needs to live.

One	More Than One
needle	needles
stem	stems
root	roots

ThinkSpeakListen

Explain how a cactus survives.

Use Language: Proper Nouns

The Coldest Place on Earth

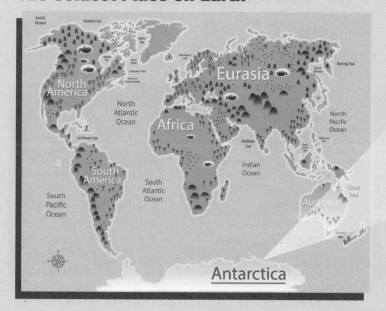

Antarctica

proper noun

Postcards from Alex

A llama named **Larry** gave me a ride up a mountain.

proper noun

A mouse named **Miguel** showed me his favorite places to eat.

proper noun

ThinkSpeakListen

Tell about the different characters in "Postcards from Alex."

49

Habitats Around the World

by Thea Feldman

A habitat is a place where plants and animals live in nature. There are different kinds of habitats around the world....

Different animals and plants live in different habitats. Let's explore a few habitats.

A grassland is one kind of habitat. Grasslands are found all over the world. Only the South Pole does not have one....

They are lands covered with grass!...

Most grasslands are flat. They cover thousands of miles.

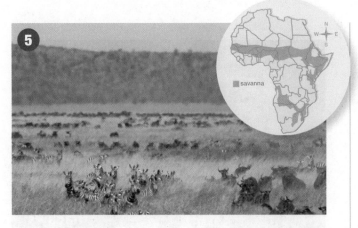

Grasslands in Africa are called savannas. A savanna has a long, hot dry season. Animals leave home each year during this season....

The animals go back home after the rainy season. The rains allow new grass to grow. The animals eat the new grass. There is also rainwater to drink....

polar bears

The world's tundras are all located near or at the North and South Poles.... In the winter, even the ground freezes!

seal
flowers
fox
oxen

In the summer, the top layer of soil thaws out. Then plants and flowers grow. Polar bears, foxes, seals, and oxen all live on the Arctic tundra.

ThinkSpeakListen

Summarize what the text is mainly about.

macaws

Nearly one-third of the planet is covered in forest habitats. There are many different kinds of forests.

A tropical rain forest is hot and rainy.... A lot of rain falls.... Trees and other plants stay green all year long.

A coral reef is a place in the ocean. It looks like a rock, but it is not. A coral reef is made of coral, a very tiny animal....

Hundreds of other kinds of animals live at a coral reef. Many sea plants live there, too. Coral reefs are found in warm, shallow water.

ThinkSpeakListen

Tell a key detail. Then tell the main idea the detail supports.

Use Language: Proper Nouns

Sentence	Proper Noun
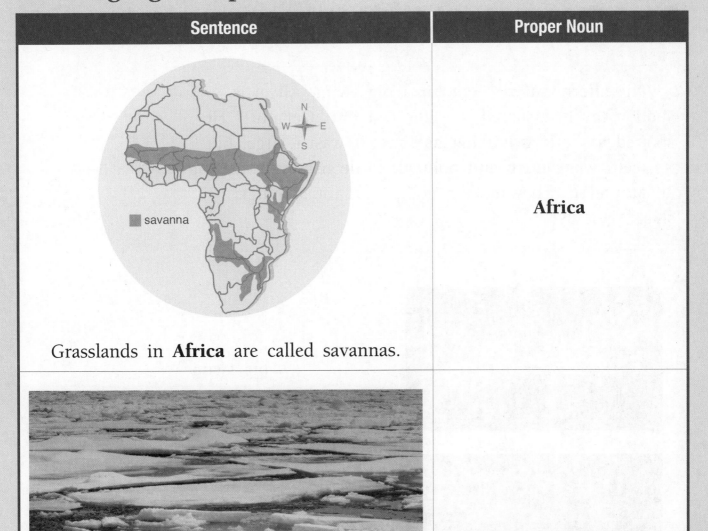 Grasslands in **Africa** are called savannas.	**Africa**
The world's tundras are all located near or at the **North** and **South Poles**.	**North** and **South Poles**

Say other nouns that tell about places and geography.

An Ocean Visit

One afternoon we went for a big swim. All of a sudden my dad started to yell, "Get out! Get out!" He spotted a shark swimming near us. It wasn't large, but its teeth were sharp and pointed. Little fish were darting all around it. They make a good meal for a hungry shark. Not us!

big swim
adjective noun

its teeth were sharp and pointed
    noun   adjective   adjective

Little fish were darting all around it.
adjective noun

ThinkSpeakListen

Describe what the author saw during the ocean visit.

Write to Sources

Drawing on "Habitats Around the World," write a short essay that explains why different animals and plants live in different habitats. Use facts and details from the reading selection as the basis for your explanation.

Type of writing

Purpose for writing

Source you will use

Sample Essay

A plant or animal lives in a habitat where it can survive the weather and find food.

— The first sentence tells the main idea.

Grasslands provide grass as food for animals that eat grass. The tundra is cold. Polar bears survive in very cold weather, and polar bears live on the tundra. Some plants and animals need the hot and rainy weather in a tropical rain forest. To survive, tiny coral needs the warm and shallow water of a coral reef.

The body text presents facts and details from the source. The details support the main idea of the essay.

Different plants and animals live in different habitats. The food and weather in a habitat allow the animals there to survive.

The conclusion reviews the main points of your essay. It provides a closing sentence.

ThinkSpeakListen

Decide on an idea. Research the text and discuss what you will write about.

Lost in the Desert

by Thea Feldman

Her mom showed Kara the map…. "Oh yeah," said Kara, as the car slowed to a stop. "The Sonoran Desert."

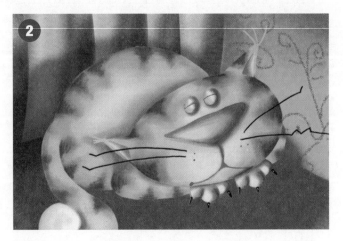

"Or, in Fred's case, the Snoring Desert!" Kara looked over at the family cat napping on the seat next to her….

Kara and her parents got out of the air-conditioned car….

"I'm glad we came early, before it gets even hotter," said Kara's mother….

She opened the car door to grab her camera…. At the same time, in the cool car, Fred woke up….

Right before Kara's mom closed the door again, he slipped outside....

Suddenly, a kangaroo rat dashed right in front of Fred and ran into the brush....

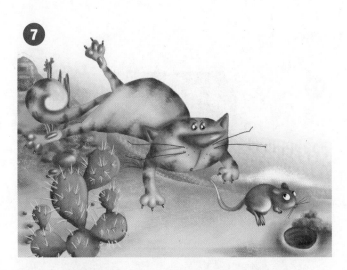

Just when Fred thought he might catch the rat, it disappeared into a hole in the ground!... The desert was quiet.

Where are the animals? Fred wondered. He did not know that most desert animals rest underground or in the shade during the day.

ThinkSpeakListen

Retell events that happen in the Sonoran Desert.

He just knew he needed to get out of the sun.... He hoped his family would realize he was missing and come back for him before it got dark....

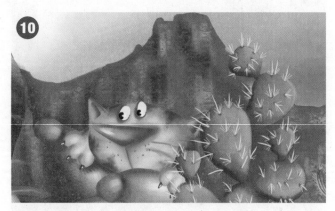

Fred licked himself. He thought it would calm him, but the desert sand in his fur just made him thirstier....

Suddenly Fred heard three car doors slam. He heard three voices call, "Fred! Fred! Fred!"... He ran toward the sounds....

Kara put a bowl of water and a dish of cat food on the car floor. "Silly Fred," she said. "Don't you know that a house cat doesn't belong in the desert?!"

ThinkSpeakListen

What happens to Fred at the end of the story?

Use Language: Analyze Shades of Meaning

Sentence	Verb	Meaning
Right before Kara's mom closed the door again, he **slipped** outside.…	**slipped**	moved in a quick and sneaky way
Suddenly, a kangaroo rat **dashed** right in front of Fred and **ran** into the brush.…	**dashed** **ran**	moved in a very quick and sudden way moved in a quick way

ThinkSpeakListen

What verb best describes how Fred is moving in the picture?

Kurt's Big Trip

Kurt and his dad went to Florida....

Noun/Verb	Linking Word	Noun/Verb
Kurt	and	his dad

His dad **turned on the engine and they took off....**

Noun/Verb	Linking Word	Noun/Verb
turned	and	took

Now they are eating all the other **plants and animals**.

Noun/Verb	Linking Word	Noun/Verb
plants	and	animals

ThinkSpeakListen

Say a sentence about one of the pictures. Use two ideas joined by the linking word "and."

Use Language: Prepositional Phrases

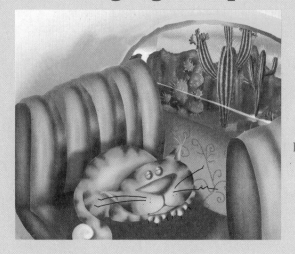

Kara looked over **at the family** cat napping
prepositional phrase
on the seat next to her....
prepositional phrase

Kara and her parents got out
of the air-conditioned car....
prepositional phrase

Suddenly, a kangaroo rat dashed right
in front of Fred and ran **into the brush**....
prepositional phrase   prepositional phrase

ThinkSpeak**Listen**

Retell what Fred does. Use a prepositional phrase.

Essential Question

How can a story change depending on who tells it?

My Language Objectives

- Use prepositional phrases
- Analyze and use adjectives and adverbs
- Use time words
- Link words and ideas
- Explain contractions
- Research and write
- Use compound nouns

My Content Objectives

- Build vocabulary related to how characters in folktales solve problems
- Understand that the person telling a story changes how the story is told

The Blind Men and the Elephant

Long ago…there lived five blind men.…

The five men were curious about many things, including nature and animals.…

…some villagers took the five men to the rajah's palace, where an elephant was kept.… He encouraged the men to examine the elephant…

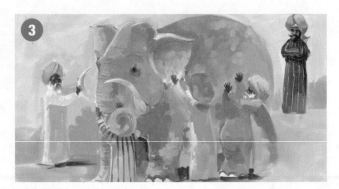

…the men began arguing… So the rajah interrupted them. "Each of you has touched only one part of the elephant," he explained.

"To know the elephant, you must put all the parts together!"

ThinkSpeakListen

Tell an event that happens in the story.

Use Language: Prepositional Phrases

Sentence	Prepositional Phrase	Preposition	Noun
Long ago, **in a village in India**, there lived five blind men.	**in a village** **in India**	**in** **in**	**village** **India**
The five men were curious **about many things**,…	**about many things**	**about**	**things**
"Each of you has touched only one part **of the elephant**," he explained.	**of the elephant**	**of**	**elephant**

The men had been blind since birth, and they had learned to rely on their other senses to understand the world.

ThinkSpeakListen

In a prepositional phrase, which is the preposition? Which is the noun?

How the Beetle Got Its Gorgeous Coat

"See how quickly I run!" the rat boasted, for he often liked to brag....

"I'm not jealous of you," the beetle replied politely....

Meanwhile, a brightly colored parrot had overheard their conversation. "I have an idea!" she exclaimed. "Let's have a race!"

"The winner will receive a unique and special prize, a brightly colored coat in colors of your choice!" she added.

The rat and beetle were excited. Both wanted a colorful coat.

Soon the race began.

The gray rat ran swiftly, as usual. *The beetle crawls so slowly*, he thought. *She can't possibly win!*

Imagine the rat's surprise when he reached the finish line and found the beetle there! "How did you do it?" he asked.

"I flew," she replied quietly and spread her wings.

"I didn't know you could fly," the rat whispered.

Then the beetle chose a gorgeous, green and gold coat—the same coat she proudly wears today!

ThinkSpeakListen

Explain to each other what the rat and the beetle do.

How Deer Got Its Horns

Long ago Deer was born with no horns. But Deer was born a good runner. His forest friend Rabbit was born a good jumper. The other animals wanted to know which could go farther faster. So they said, "Let's have a race!"

But Deer was born a <u>good</u> <u>runner</u>.

       adjective   noun

His forest friend Rabbit was born a <u>good</u> jumper.

adjective   noun

The other animals wanted to know which could <u>go</u> <u>farther</u> <u>faster</u>.

       verb   adverb   adverb

ThinkSpeakListen

Say a new sentence with an adjective that describes a noun.

Use Language: Time Words

The Blind Men and the Elephant

Sentence	Time Words
Long ago, in a village in India, there lived five blind men.	**long ago**
One day, some villagers took the five men to the rajah's palace, where an elephant was kept.	**one day**

How the Beetle Got Its Gorgeous Coat

Sentence	Time Words
Meanwhile, a brightly colored parrot had overheard their conversation.	**meanwhile**
Then the beetle chose a gorgeous, green and gold coat—the same coat she proudly wears today!	**then**

ThinkSpeakListen
Use time words to tell about a story event you just read.

Stone Soup

retold by Winston Ramos

Late one evening, long ago, an old man walked into a village....

"I am looking for a place for the night, and a meal to share," he said.

"You have come to the wrong place, stranger," said a woman....

"I am sorry," said another villager. "There is not enough food for ourselves."...

"I was not asking for food," said the old man. "I was thinking of making some stone soup to share with you."...

Then, with a quick move, like a magician, he pulled a large pot from his coat. The hungry villagers watched as he filled the pot with water....

When the water was boiling, he reached into his coat again. This time he took a large stone from a velvet bag. He dropped the stone into the pot....

"Is the stone soup really for everyone?" asked the boy.

"It is for anyone who wants it," said the old man....

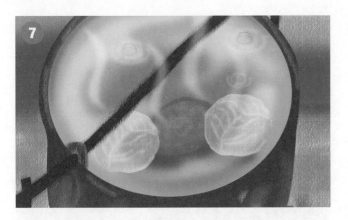

"Of course, stone soup with cabbage is even better!"

Soon, a villager approached with a cabbage.... He added the cabbage to the pot....

Soon after that the village butcher came..."I was saving this small leg of lamb for my Sunday dinner."... He dropped the lamb into the pot....

ThinkSpeakListen

Tell the story's main idea. Give a detail that supports the main idea.

In no time at all, several villagers found a turnip or carrot and added them to the soup....

Before long a delicious meal was ready.

Everyone in the village who wanted stone soup had a big bowlful.

No one went to bed hungry that night.

The next day, the villagers begged the old man to stay. But he needed to move on. Before leaving...he shared his secret with the village elders.

The villagers learned the magic of sharing and they never went hungry again.

ThinkSpeakListen

Discuss the lesson that the villagers learn from the old man.

Use Language: Link Words and Ideas

Idea	Linking Word	Idea
In no time at all, several villagers found a turnip or carrot	**and**	added them to the soup.
The villagers learned the magic of sharing	**and**	they never went hungry again.

ThinkSpeakListen
Talk about the picture of the old man. Use "and" to link two ideas.

City Mouse and Country Mouse

"Oh dear," said the city mouse. "This place isn't like my home."

"You don't like it?" asked the country mouse.

"I like the clear, blue skies. But I don't like the food here," the city mouse replied. "Let's go to the city. I have many more things to eat!" So the two mice went to the city.

	Contraction	Meaning
	This place **isn't** like my home.	is not
	You **don't** like it?	do not
	Let's go to the city.	let us

ThinkSpeakListen

Use each contraction on the chart in a new sentence.

Research and Write

Imagine that you have been asked to write a folktale about stone soup from the point of view of the boy. What other stories have characters with points of view similar to the villagers'? Read and take notes from two or more approved digital sources to answer this question. List the sources of your information.

Research

Write

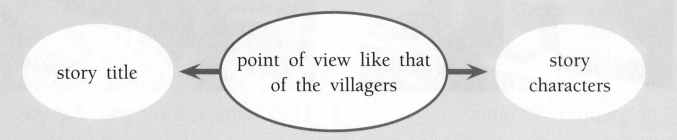

My Research Findings

Story	Characters	Point of View
Cactus Soup, by Eric A. Kimmel www.nypl.org	soldiers	hungry and want food
	Capitán	tricks the townspeople into giving food by making soup with a cactus needle
	townspeople	do not want to share their food, and hide their tamales, tortillas, and beans
Kallaloo! by David and Phillis Gershator www.nypl.org	Granny	hungry and has no money tricks the people of Market Square into making soup with a seashell
	the people of Market Square	tricked into giving Granny food because she says her shell is magic all enjoy the soup in the end

The Stone Garden:
A reimagining of "Stone Soup" by Jeffrey Fuerst

The people of Yancy Place were proud of their neighborhood.

That changed when the gas station on the corner closed.

The owners took out the gas tanks....

"This is an eyesore!" said the people of Yancy Place.... "What can be done about it?"...

An old man in a cloth cap stepped through the crowd.... "This is not an eyesore," he said. "It is a lovely stone garden."...

He pushed a large stone to the center of the lot....

"Let me put some rocks around the big stone. Then you will see the makings of a fine stone garden."...

5

"Of course," he said, "to make this stone garden world-class, we might paint the rocks different colors."…

6

"I have some red paint," said the woman with the dog.

"I have some blue paint," volunteered another person.

7

Within an hour, the little rocks around the big stone glowed. They were painted with every color of the rainbow. "Yes indeed," said the visitor.…

8

"Of course, to make a stone garden a garden, it should have plants. It should have flowers."

A girl made her way through the crowd.…

ThinkSpeakListen

Tell events that happen in the story.

"I am growing tomatoes in flowerpots at home. I can bring in some seedlings."…

"My cousin works in a flower shop," said another person.…

"I don't mind getting my hands dirty," said a young man.…

"Sign us up," said some teenagers.…

The people of Yancy Place worked all day in the garden. They worked the next day, too.…

By that time, the old man had on his backpack. He took one last look at one of the truly finest stone gardens he had ever seen, and was on his way.

ThinkSpeakListen

Discuss how the old man helps the people of Yancy Place.

Use Language: Adjectives

Let me put <u>some</u> <u>rocks</u> around the <u>big</u> <u>stone</u>.
adjective   noun   adjective noun

I have some <u>blue</u> <u>paint</u>.
adjective   noun

The people of Yancy Place worked <u>all</u>
<u>day</u> in the garden.   adjective
noun

ThinkSpeakListen

Say a sentence that uses an adjective with a noun.

Goldilocks and the Three Bears

Goldilocks spotted three bowls of porridge. The big bowl was too hot. The medium bowl was too cold. The little bowl was just right. She ate it all.

Then she spotted three chairs. The big chair was too hard. The medium chair was too soft. The little chair was just right. So she sat in it. *Splat!* The chair broke into little bits.

too hot
adverb adjective

too cold
adverb adjective

just right
adverb adjective

ThinkSpeakListen

Find adverbs in the paragraph that tell *how much* about an adjective.

Use Language: Compound Nouns

Sentence	Compound Noun
 "This is an eyesore!" said the people of Yancy Place.	eye + sore = eyesore
 They were painted with every color of the rainbow.	rain + bow = rainbow
 "I am growing tomatoes in flowerpots at home."	flower + pots = flowerpots

ThinkSpeakListen

Make up a new sentence that uses the noun *flowerpots*.

Essential Question

Where do ideas for inventions come from?

My Language Objectives

- Use adjectives
- Use past tense verbs
- Use multiple-meaning words
- Use irregular adjectives
- Use technology nouns

My Content Objectives

- Build vocabulary related to where ideas come from
- Understand how ideas change our everyday lives

A Woman with Vision

Years ago, drivers had no way to see through their windshield when snow and rain obscured their vision....

In 1903, Mary Anderson was riding in a streetcar in unpleasant weather. She noticed drivers constantly stopping to scrape and rescrape their windshields....

She invented a window-clearing device that drivers controlled from inside their cars.

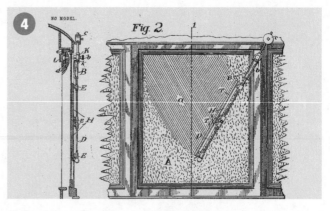

Those first wipers were manual, not motorized. But they changed cars and driving forever.

ThinkSpeakListen
Retell the main idea of this page.

Use Language: Adjectives

unpleasant weather
adjective   noun

a better way
adjective noun

first wipers
adjective noun

ThinkSpeakListen

One partner says a noun, the other says an adjective that goes with it.

A Lucky Accident

George de Mestral found his invention by accident. After walking outdoors, George's overcoat and his dog's fur were covered in prickly plants called burrs.

George wondered what made their grip so strong. He looked closely. He noticed tiny hooks on the burrs.

George found that those hooks caught on anything with loops, such as fabric, or cloth, and fur. That hook-and-loop discovery became famous....

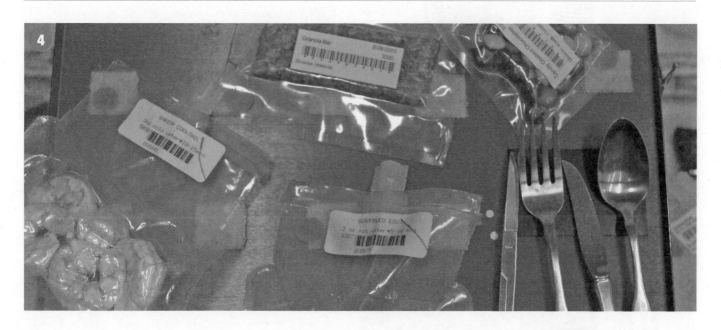

But almost everyone can press and pull this sticky fabric. Astronauts even use it to hold down stuff in space!

ThinkSpeakListen

Summarize how George de Mestral invented the hook-and-loop fabric.

Kid Inventors

Hart Main is a kid inventor. He didn't like his sister's candles. They smelled like things only girls would like. So he said, "I'll invent candles for boys!" He got wax and stuff to make different scents, or smells. Then he got old soup cans. He made candles that smelled like coffee, bacon, baseball mitts, and freshly cut grass. They were a big hit!

old soup cans
adjective adjective   noun

baseball mitts
adjective   noun

freshly cut grass
adverb   adjective   noun

ThinkSpeakListen

Say a sentence that has three new smells for candles.

Use Language: Past Tense Verbs

A Woman with Vision

Sentence		Present Tense Verb	Past Tense Verb
	Drivers had no way to see through their windshield when snow and rain **obscured** their vision.	obscure	obscur**ed**
	She **invented** a window-clearing device.	invent	invent**ed**

A Lucky Accident

Sentence		Present Tense Verb	Past Tense Verb
	George **wondered** what made their grip so strong.	wonder	wonder**ed**
	He **noticed** tiny hooks on the burrs.	notice	notic**ed**

ThinkSpeakListen

Use past tense verbs to talk about the picture above.

Famous Inventors

by Margaret McNamara

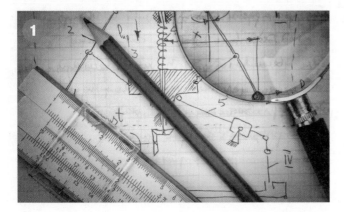

An inventor is someone who creates something new. An inventor also finds new ways to do things. An inventor works to solve problems.

Get ready to meet and read about three famous inventors.... See how their inventions changed the way people live every day.

Thomas Alva Edison loved to read and to learn.... He made improvements to a machine used by the stock market....

Edison decided to become a full-time inventor.... During his lifetime, Edison and his workers came up with more than 1,000 inventions.

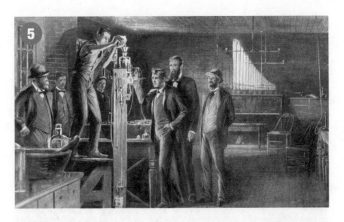

5

He is best known for inventing the first long-lasting electric lightbulb. He also invented the phonograph…. He invented the first movie camera, too….

6

Alexander Graham Bell had a lifelong interest in communication…. In 1872, Bell began to tutor deaf children. He also worked to make a better telegraph.

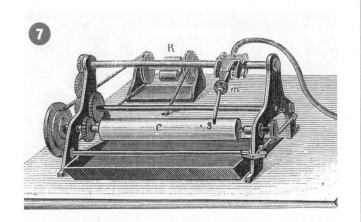

7

A telegraph sends and receives coded sound messages. The sounds were beeps and clicks. Each sound stood for a letter….

8

Bell wanted to invent a machine that would send and receive the human voice…. In 1876, Bell showed the world the first telephone….

ThinkSpeakListen

Tell which of the inventions on this page we still use today.

George Washington Carver was an African American. He was born a slave in Missouri.... He was the first black student at Iowa State Agricultural College....

After college, Carver became a teacher. He taught students and farmers about plants....

Carver taught farmers how to grow peanut plants.... He invented hundreds of new uses for peanuts and sweet potatoes....

Some inventors make things that change the way people live.... The inventors in this book all changed the world for the better.

ThinkSpeakListen

Describe one thing each of these three inventors invented.

Use Language: Multiple-Meaning Words

Sentence	Meaning	Second Meaning
Each sound stood for a **letter**.	A part of the alphabet	a written message
He **spotted** some geese.	saw	blotched, like a leopard
Would they **hatch**, too?	break open	opening on a ship's deck
A telegraph sends and receives coded **sound** messages.	noise	a body of water

ThinkSpeakListen

Use one of the words in two sentences to show the different meanings.

The Curious Boy

Sentence	Present Tense Verb	Irregular Past Tense Verb
Thomas Edison **was** a curious boy.	is	was
He wondered, if people **ate** worms, could they fly, too?	eat	ate
Tom placed a few eggs in the nest and **sat** down.	sit	sat
When he couldn't get answers, he **did** experiments.	do	did
Finding the answers to his questions **brought** him great joy.	bring	brought

ThinkSpeakListen

Say a sentence with one of the irregular past tense verbs in the chart.

Use Language: Irregular Adjectives

In 1872, Bell began to tutor deaf children.
He also worked to make a better telegraph.

Irregular Adjective	Comparative	Superlative
good	better	best
bad	worse	worst

ThinkSpeakListen

Describe an invention. Use one of the adjectives above.

Robots Go to School by Kathy Kafer

It's a school morning. Drew wakes up and gets dressed.... But instead of getting on the school bus, he turns on his computer. Drew stays home and sends his robot to school....

Special robots now go to school for some children.... Most of these children are too sick to go to school....

Nate hears the teacher talk. He can also hear what the other students say. From the hospital, Nate can ask questions. He can talk to his friends.

The robot has a video screen.... If he wants to answer a question, he presses a button. A light flashes on the robot. The teacher knows to call on Nate.

The robot has wheels.... It can travel up and down the hallways.... The robot can even line up with the other children during a fire drill....

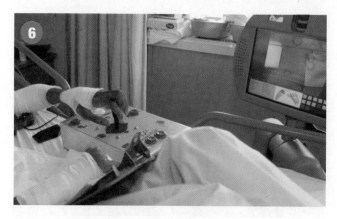

Nate moves the robot with his computer mouse. A signal is sent through the Internet to the robot. And the robot sends videos back to Nate.

The children who use school robots often give them nicknames.... The robot might wear the child's favorite T-shirt or bright ribbons....

The other children...often forget that the robot is a robot. Instead, they just see their friend....

ThinkSpeakListen

Describe how a school robot can help a student.

The robots let teachers keep in touch with their sick students. Teachers can even give classroom jobs to children at home....

Of course, school robots are not real children. They cannot think or talk on their own. They don't learn for the children who use them....

The robots have limitations. They cannot climb stairs or open doors.... When the Internet is down, the sick child cannot tell the robot what to do....

A school robot comes with a high price: $6,000. People are working to lower the cost. They are also making these special robots better.

ThinkSpeakListen

Discuss this question: What must students do that their robots cannot?

Use Language: Technology Nouns

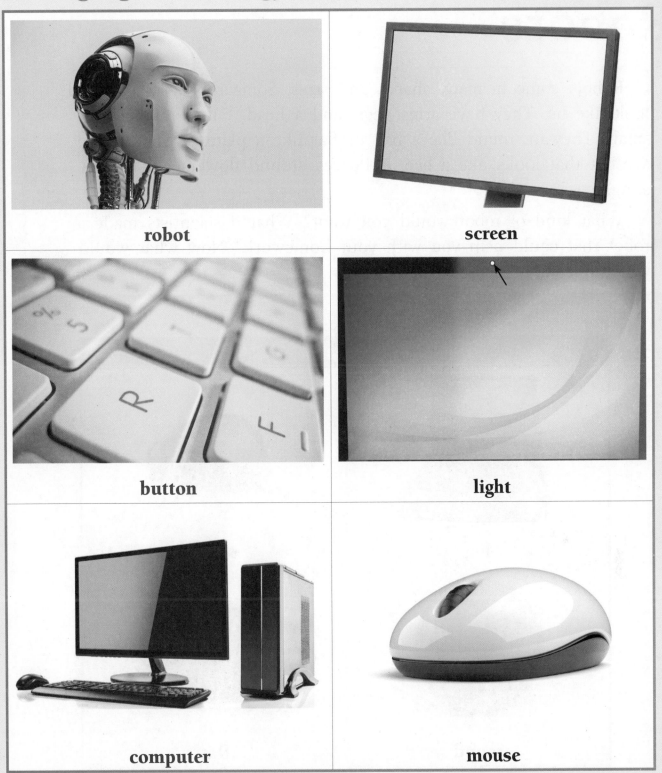

robot

screen

button

light

computer

mouse

ThinkSpeakListen

Explain how you use technology at school.

Robots

Robots come in many shapes and sizes. Some robots are big and look like us. They have arms, legs, and a head. Other robots are small. They are round like a ball or flat like a plate.... There's also a robot that looks like a bee. It buzzes around flowers but doesn't sting....

What kind of robot would you want? What if scientists made a robot that could help you with your homework? Now what would you think about that?

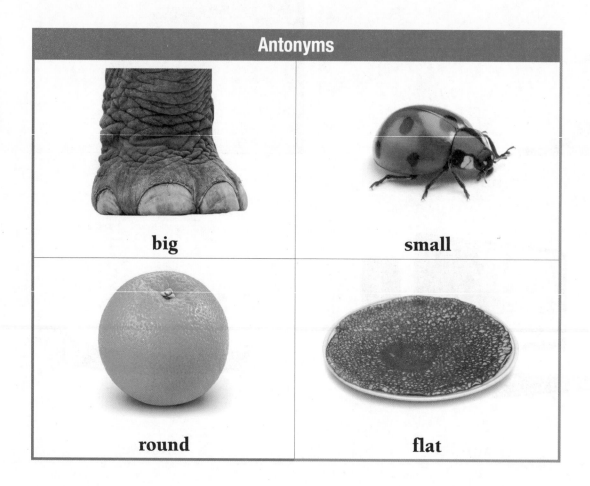

Antonyms

| big | small |
| round | flat |

ThinkSpeakListen

Describe two different robots. Use words that are antonyms.

Write to Sources

Of all the inventions you read about in this unit, which do you think has been the most helpful to people's lives? Why? In a short essay, state your opinion and provide reasons to support it. Use evidence from two of the reading selections to support your opinion and reasons.

Type of writing

Purpose for writing

Source you will use

Sample Essay

The most important of all these inventions was Alexander Graham Bell's telephone.

The telephone is the basis for how people talk and communicate today. According to "Famous Inventors," in 1876, Bell showed the world the first telephone. People in different places could now hear one another's voices. The text also says "Some inventors make things that change the way people live."

Inventions change how people live. The most important ones change something basic, like how we talk to each other. No matter how much things change, the need to talk to each other faster, better, and easier will never go away.

The first sentence states the opinion.

The body presents reasons.
The reasons support the opinion of the essay.
The text provides evidence to support the opinion and reasons.

The conclusion reviews the main points of your essay. It provides a closing sentence.

What can different cultures teach us?

My Language Objectives

- Use irregular past tense verbs
- Use adjectives that compare
- Describe with adjectives
- Use informal English
- Use nouns

My Content Objectives

- Build vocabulary related to folktales from different cultures
- Understand what different cultures can teach

Why the Sky Is Far Away

1. Many years ago, the sky was very close to our Earth. People could reach up, break off a piece of the sky, and eat it!…

2. The sky…spoke to the people. "You are wasting my precious gift of food. If you continue to do that, I will go away!"…

3. …the people…forgot all about the sky's warning…. The sky saw everything and said, "You are greedy and wasteful. Now I will go far away."

4. "But how will we eat?" asked the people.

"You will work for your food by planting crops," the sky replied. Then the sky floated up high, where it is today.

ThinkSpeakListen
Retell the folktale.

Use Language: Irregular Past Tense Verbs

Sentence	Present Tense Verb	Irregular Past Tense Verb
Many years ago, the sky **was** very close to our Earth. People could reach up, break off a piece of the sky, and eat it!	**is**	**was**
The sky…**spoke** to the people.	**speak**	**spoke**
They **broke** off huge pieces of the sky.	**break**	**broke**

ThinkSpeakListen

Describe a scene from the story using past tense verbs.

King Midas

The king was fond of gold and loved it more than anything, except his daughter, Marigold.

One day, as King Midas counted his coins, a stranger appeared.

"If I could grant you one wish, what would it be?" he asked.

"I'd wish that everything I touched turned into gold," King Midas replied....

The next morning, the king awoke earlier than usual....

He was delighted and thrilled when everything he touched became gold!...

Then Marigold ran to him. But when he embraced her with a kiss, she became a golden statue!

106

"What have I done?" the king cried. And he wept with grief and sorrow.

Suddenly, the stranger appeared before him.

"You look like the saddest man in the land," said the stranger.

"I've lost everything I care about," sobbed the king.

"Fill this pitcher with water from the lake," instructed the stranger. "Then sprinkle it on everything you've turned to gold."

King Midas followed his instructions. When everything returned to normal, the king was the happiest man ever!

ThinkSpeakListen

Explain what happens in this story.

Mercury and the Ax

A young man went to the forest to chop down a tree. It was June and the hot noon sun beat down on him. His hands started to sweat. The ax flew out of his loose hands and landed in the river. The man began to cry. "My ax might not have been new, but it was all I had. It is lost forever."

Idea	Linking Word	Idea
It was June	**and**	the hot noon sun beat down on him.
"My ax might not have been new,	**but**	it was all I had."

ThinkSpeakListen

Choose a picture on this page. Make up a new sentence about it. Use the word "and" or "but" to link two ideas.

Use Language: Adjectives That Compare
King Midas

Sentence	Adjective	Adjective Meaning *More*	Adjective Meaning *Most*
Long ago, there lived a king named Midas who was the **richest** man in the land.	**rich**	**rich<u>er</u>**	**rich<u>est</u>**
The next morning, the king awoke **earlier** than usual.	**early**	**earli<u>er</u>**	**earli<u>est</u>**
"You look like the **saddest** man in the land," said the stranger.	**sad**	**sadd<u>er</u>**	**sadd<u>est</u>**

ThinkSpeakListen
Explain why the stranger says that King Midas looks like "the saddest man in the land."

A Foxy Garden

by Jeffrey Fuerst

Bear found...ripe blueberry bushes by the creek. He stuffed himself with berries and...fell asleep. Squirrel and Rabbit followed their noses to the blueberry patch, too....

"Hey!" growled Bear. "Those are MY blueberries."...

Squirrel and Rabbit hightailed it...to the woods where they told their wise friend Fox...

"Bear is being his usual selfish self," said Fox. "We'll have to do something about that."

Fox grabbed a handful of special, fast-growing seeds.

Then he went to Bear... "We'll share"... said Fox. "You can have everything that grows above the ground. I will get everything that grows below the ground."...

"How about we grow carrots?" Fox suggested…. Bear and Fox dug holes for the carrot seeds…. The seeds grew….

Fox took the carrots, cut off the green tops, and gave them to Bear….

"Hey!" said Bear. "The green tops are not good for eating. I want the orange part."

"Ah," said Fox, "the orange part is the root. It grows below the ground."…

"Okay," said Fox. "How about celery?"…

Bear and Fox planted and watered the celery seeds…. After a while, the celery was ready….

Fox cut off the thick stems that grew above the ground….

"Ugh" said Bear biting into the bitter celery root….

ThinkSpeakListen

How does Fox feel about the garden he and Bear grow together? How does Bear feel?

"This time let's plant another garden. I will get the roots and the stems!"

"Okay," said Fox. "How about something that makes a good salad?"…

Bear and Fox planted and watered lettuce seeds.…

Bear picked armfuls of lettuce.…

"Not so fast," said Fox. "You said you would get the roots and the stems."…

"I will make a lettuce, carrot, and celery salad. I will invite Squirrel and Rabbit."…

Bear stormed off to the blueberry bushes by the creek.…

Soon, sadness pushed aside anger…Bear felt left out.…

"I was wrong not to share the berries," said Bear. "Here is a basket for each of you."

ThinkSpeakListen
What does Bear do at the end of the story? Why?

112

Use Language: Describe with Adjectives

Fox grabbed a handful of <u>special</u>, <u>fast-growing</u> <u>seeds</u>.
                                  adjective   adjective   noun

"Ah," said Fox, "the <u>orange</u> <u>part</u> is the root."
                         adjective noun

"How about something that makes a <u>good</u> <u>salad</u>?"
                                       adjective noun

"I will make a <u>lettuce</u>, <u>carrot</u>, and <u>celery</u> <u>salad</u>."
                       adjective adjective   adjective noun

ThinkSpeakListen

Make up a new sentence about salad. Add a new adjective that describes something about the salad.

The Many Tales of Red Riding Hood

In Africa, kids hear about a girl named Pretty Salma. She runs into Big Bad Dog on her way to the market. He tricks her and dresses as her grandmother. With the help of Anansi the spider, she saves the day.

	Sentence	Pronoun = Noun
	She runs into Big Bad Dog on **her** way to the market.	she = Pretty Salma her = Pretty Salma
	He tricks her and dresses as her grandmother.	he = Big Bad Dog

ThinkSpeakListen
Retell what happens to Pretty Salma.

Use Language: Informal English

Sentence	Informal English Word
"**Hey!**" growled Bear.	**hey**
"**Ah**," said Fox, "the orange part is the root."	**ah**
"**Okay**," said Fox.	**okay**
"**Ugh**," said Bear, biting into the bitter celery root.	**ugh**

ThinkSpeakListen

Make up a sentence that a character in a story might say. Use an informal English word.

On One Wheel by Carly Schuna

"Martha, please take Casey to the nurse," said Ms. Perkins.

"So, you're not a dodgeball player," said Martha as we walked down the hall. "What are you good at?"

"Well," I admitted, "I'm just not very good at normal sports."…

How was I going to make friends if I couldn't even play the sports we did in gym class?

"Mom," I said as I got into the car later, "I can't do anything!"…

"You're the only kid at unicycle club who can wheel walk," Mom added….

Mom was right—I am awesome on the unicycle.…

That night, I had a dream. It was gym class, and we were playing basketball.

Instead of throwing balls at the basket, though, everybody was throwing them at me....

Then my unicycle flew down from the sky....

I woke up with an idea. "Can I ride my unicycle to school today?" I asked Mom...

"Hmm," she said. "...if I ride my bike next to you."...

"Whoa," somebody said. "You can ride a unicycle?"

Then I saw Martha looking right at me. I hopped off my unicycle.

"What is that?" asked Martha. "Did you lose half your bicycle or something?"...

"This is my unicycle. I ride with a club."...

ThinkSpeakListen
Who is telling the story? How do you know?

117

9

"Can I try?" asked Martha….

Mom stood on one side of the unicycle and helped Martha up….

10

Martha tried to pedal forward, but she fell off the unicycle right away. A couple of kids snickered….

"Want to try again?"…

11

Martha looked at me. "Can I see you do it again?" she asked….

I hopped on my unicycle and zoomed around forward and backward.

12

Then I took my feet off the pedals and did my wheel walk….

Martha giggled, and I grinned. Maybe making friends wouldn't be so bad after all.

ThinkSpeakListen
Explain how this story ends.

Use Language: Nouns

basketball

dodgeball

unicycle

ThinkSpeakListen

Describe a sport you like.

No Small Trick

Sentence	Preposition	Noun
I go to a special school **in the city**.	in	city
We have kids **from all over the world**.	from	world
After lunch, we like to do one thing: Play ball.	after	lunch
We played together **on the weekends**.	on	weekends

ThinkSpeakListen

Make up a new sentence about the picture above. Use a prepositional phrase.

Write to Sources

After reading "On One Wheel," reread "A Foxy Garden." Both stories have characters that learn lessons. Choose one character from each story and write a short essay that explains why you think these characters needed to learn a lesson. Use evidence from both texts to support your opinion and reasons.

Type of writing

Purpose for writing

Source you will use

Sample Essay

Bear and Casey needed to learn a lesson. Each character had a different lesson to learn.

Bear was selfish and wanted food all to himself. He did not give blueberries to Squirrel and Rabbit. But he wanted Fox to give him carrots, celery, and lettuce.

Casey was afraid she would not make friends in her new school because she wasn't good at popular sports. She could ride a unicycle, but that was an unusual sport.

Both characters learned important lessons. Bear learned to share food and be friendly with the other animals. Casey learned that she could make friends by being herself. They both learned something important about friendship.

The first sentence states the opinion.

The body presents reasons. The reasons support the opinion of the essay. The text provides evidence to support the opinion and reasons.

The conclusion restates the main points of your essay. It provides a closing sentence.

ThinkSpeakListen

Think about the characters in the two stories you read. Which characters needed to learn a lesson? Decide on your opinion.

Essential Question

How does understanding the past shape the future?

NEWS

Economic Growth Picks Up

This year, all over Europe and Central Asia, emerging economies are expected to grow. It was noted that some countries in the region could be seriously affected by rising food and energy prices. Major oil exporters, which account for 15 percent of the entire world's oil, are benefiting from price increase and it contributes to economic growth and stability of the budget balance.

However, rising prices for food and fuel prices creates an additional source of vulnerability for many importing countries, noted at a press conference. In response, governments in the region proposed to increase the coverage and targeting of social protection systems to support the poor. Recommend avoiding some of the measures that were taken in the region in response to previous price increases for energy and food - such as price controls and restrictions on foreign trade and export of food. pecialists drew attention to a new problem - the growth in commodity prices, which turned out to be more significant than expected. The growth in food prices is even more serious problem in emerging markets, where central banks do not enjoy a special trust. Therefore, in these countries, they should be more careful. It is possible that for some time, the level of inflation will be somewhat higher than expected. However, according to our forecasts, we do not think that it will have a severe negative impact on economic growth. High prices for raw materials may pose a real threat to the developing countries,

Real estate market review

This year as a whole is expected to steady but slight growth. This means that in most real estate markets will dominate the cautious mood. According to experts, renters are unlikely to seek significant investment, and actively expand in the face of uncertainty. So, they want to see evidence of the resumption of sustained growth around the world before the deal with the extension. So that the base rental rates in most major business centers in the following year will remain at about the same level as that in the past. According to the forecast, this year is possible and a marked increase in base rental rates in some cities, applying the appropriate expectations. With regard to the effect that economic growth will have on demand for space by renters in the near future, experts believe that the decisions taken by companies lease refer to the long term. In addition, the experts reviewed the changes that have occurred in the property market over the past year.

Oil prices hit two-year high

The other day trades in oil contracts reached a 2-year high not seen since September 2008, and amounted to $ 108 per barrel. At the stock exchange price of crude oil decisively crossed the $ 120 per barrel, and the trades have not only held within close to the 2-year high, but often exceeding the record level. At present, European refineries are in a difficult position due to lack of supplied raw materials, which became one of the reasons for the increase in prices for their products. As evidenced by past expe-

My Language Objectives

- Use cause and effect signal words
- Use verbs
- Determine multiple-meaning words
- Use compound words
- Use adjectives

My Content Objectives

- Build vocabulary related to learning about the past
- Understand how the past shapes our future

schoolhouse
of the past

schoolhouse
of the present

The Oregon Trail

1
May 17, 1849

Dear Diary,

Papa and I walk while Mama and the baby ride. Papa says it's because our weight would be too much for the mules....

2
June 29, 1849

Rain, rain, and more rain!... Today our wagon got stuck in the mud. As a result, a wheel broke. It was another setback....

3
July 14, 1849

Sunrise brought a magnificent sight—a herd of buffalo grazing on the plain. Our provisions have been getting low, so we stopped at an Indian village....

4
August 1, 1849

We have arrived at Soda Springs!... We are going to stay here for an extra day because we need the rest....

Yours truly, Edith

ThinkSpeakListen

Which event in the diary do you think is the most important? Why?

Use Language: Cause and Effect Signal Words

Today our wagon got stuck in the mud. As a result, a wheel broke.
<u>cause</u>   <u>signal words</u>   <u>effect</u>

We are going to stay here for an extra day because we need the rest.
<u>effect</u>   <u>signal word</u>   <u>cause</u>

Our provisions have been getting low, so we stopped at an Indian village.
<u>cause</u>   <u>signal word</u>   <u>effect</u>

Papa and I walk... Papa says it's because our weight would be too much for the mules.
<u>effect</u>   <u>signal word</u>   <u>cause</u>

ThinkSpeakListen

Explain why the narrator and her father cannot ride on the mules.

Helen Keller: Words through Touch

A childhood illness left Helen Keller deaf and blind. One of the ways she learned about the world was through touch. This is what she wrote:

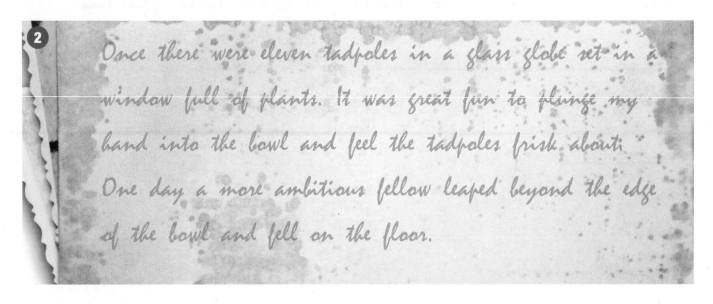

Once there were eleven tadpoles in a glass globe set in a window full of plants. It was great fun to plunge my hand into the bowl and feel the tadpoles frisk about.

One day a more ambitious fellow leaped beyond the
edge of the bowl and fell on the floor. I found him
more dead than alive.

But no sooner had he returned to his element than he
darted to the bottom, swimming round and round. Then
he went to live in the leafy pool at the end of the garden.

ThinkSpeakListen
Tell what happens first, next, and last.

127

Dear Diary

June 4, 1860

Mama, Papa, and I heard a knock on our door one night. That was our sign that it was safe to leave. We met a woman named Harriet Tubman. She came to lead us north to freedom. Since it was <u>nighttime</u> and not safe to go by <u>candlelight</u>, we used the <u>moonlight</u> to see. It was important that no one make a sound. No talking! If we got caught, we would be sent back to slavery, or worse. I have never been so scared.

Mama packed some <u>cornbread</u> in a knapsack for us to eat. We went mostly on foot. We stopped at safe houses along the way for food and rest. Few children make this trip, so I knew I was lucky. It was a long trip on the <u>Underground Railroad</u>. We are in the North now, and we are FREE!

Harriet Tubman

Compound Words	
night + time = nighttime	corn + bread = cornbread
candle + light = candlelight	under + ground = underground
moon + light = moonlight	rail + road = railroad

ThinkSpeakListen

Retell key details from the narrator's diary.

Use Language: Verbs

Helen Keller: Words through Touch

Sentence	Verb	Meaning
It was great fun to **plunge** my hand into the bowl and feel the tadpoles **frisk** about.	**plunge**	dive in
	frisk	jump around playfully
But no sooner had he returned to his element than he **darted** to the bottom…	**darted**	moved quickly

The Oregon Trail

Sentence	Verb	Meaning
Sunrise brought a magnificent sight—a herd of buffalo **grazing** on the plain.	**grazing**	eating

ThinkSpeakListen

Tell what is happening in one of the pictures above.

Primary Sources

by Margaret McNamara

How do you find out about... the past? One of the best ways is to find primary sources.... A primary source is someone who has direct knowledge of the topic....

You can also look for paintings, photographs, writings, and artifacts.... An interview is when you ask someone questions....

A reporter's interview is a primary source.... You can listen to some interviews on the radio or the Internet. You can read other interviews in newspapers or in magazines.

Photography did not exist until the 1800s. Before then, people painted and drew pictures... These paintings are primary sources of information....

Photography quickly became an important way to record events. Almost every major event from the 1900s to today has been captured in photos.

Photographs are good primary sources for topics from the past. They are good primary sources for things that happen today, too.

The written word...is one of the oldest primary sources. In the past, people sent handwritten letters to one another....

Diaries, newspapers, and documents are other forms of the written word. They are good ways to learn about the past.

ThinkSpeakListen

Tell what you might learn from the photo of Martin Luther King Jr.

9

Artifacts are things made by people.... We can learn about how people lived and worked by looking at old tools.

10

Artifacts show what daily life was like in the past. Old toys tell us how people used to have fun!

11

A primary source is directly connected to the topic you are researching. A primary source offers firsthand knowledge...

12

Once you decide on a topic, primary sources will get you started on your journey into the past.

ThinkSpeakListen

Say what one of the artifacts tells you about the people who used it.

Use Language: Multiple-Meaning Words

Sentence	Meaning	Possible Other Meaning
You **can** interview that person about the event.	**can** able to	**can** a metal container
What he or she says may **lead** you to ask new questions.	**lead** guide	**lead** a heavy metal
Photography quickly became an important way to **record** events.	**record** capture	**record** a vinyl disk with music on it
They **show** how people lived long ago.	**show** demonstrate	**show** a performance
Primary sources **will** get you started.	**will** shall	a written document

ThinkSpeakListen

Say a sentence that shows the other meaning of one of the words above.

Grandpa's Treasure Chest

In another photo, Grandpa was riding to town on a horse. Dad said they didn't have cars when Grandpa was young. Grandpa loved taking horseback rides. Back then, they had no TV, no computers, no video games. They rode horses for fun. I think I would have liked riding horses, too.

Nouns

photo

computers

cars

horse

ThinkSpeakListen

Describe how life in Grandpa's time was different from life today.

Use Language: Compound Words

A primary source offers <u>firsthand</u> knowledge
of a topic.

compound

Diaries, <u>newspapers</u>, and documents are
other forms of the written word.

compound

In the past, people sent <u>handwritten</u> letters
to one another.

compound

ThinkSpeakListen

Explain why firsthand knowledge is important.

A Dinosaur Named SUE:
A Journal About My Summer Dig by Terri Patterson

1 August 11, 1990

Tomorrow is the last day of the dig.... It's been a long, hot, but great summer. We dug up many dinosaur bones. Some are more than sixty million years old!...

2 August 12, 1990

We are here.

What a day!... Sue...found some huge bones sticking out of a cliff. They were too big to be anything but a dinosaur.... In this part of the world, it could only be a T. rex!...

3

The ground...was covered with pieces of bone.... Pete thought that a whole skeleton might be buried there. He named the dinosaur SUE after the person who found it.

4

We only have one problem right now. The bones are under almost thirty feet of dirt and rock. It's going to take a lot of hard work to remove...

5 August 14, 1990

Early this morning, we started digging up the T. rex.... A machine might break or crush the fossils, so we did all the work by hand.... We used picks to break up smaller rocks and shovels to move dirt....

6 August 18, 1990

Our hard work over the past few days finally paid off. Today we got down to the fossils.... We used small hand tools to remove the dirt and rock around the bones....

7 August 23, 1990

Pete dug out the skull today. It's almost five feet long! He thinks that this T. rex was a giant. Its bones are bigger than any T. rex he has seen....

8

We took pictures as we worked. It's important to record the positions of the bones.... We also found fossils of plants and other dinosaurs....

ThinkSpeakListen

Say why different parts of the dig need different tools.

9 **August 29, 1990**

As we dug up bones...we left some rock around them.... Weak bones get special care. They get a thin coat of glue and layers of tinfoil. Then we wrap them in a plaster cast....

10 **September 1, 1990**

We left the dig today. It took seventeen days to dig SUE out of the ground. All the bones are finally on their way to the lab. It will take a long time to clean up the skeleton....

11 **May 17, 2000**

This journal has been in a box for almost ten years... I pulled it out tonight to add one last entry.... The T. rex is now on display in Chicago....

12

Scientists can keep studying the bones. And people from around the world can visit the largest and most complete T. rex ever found.

ThinkSpeakListen

Explain why it is important to preserve dinosaur bones.

Use Language: Adjectives

Weak bones get special care.
adjective noun   adjective noun

Then we wrap them in a plaster cast.
                                    adjective noun

Our hard work over the past few days
     adjective noun   adjective adjective noun
finally paid off.

People from around the world can visit
the largest and most complete T. rex
    adjective   adjective adjective   noun
ever found.

ThinkSpeakListen

Describe how the scientists protect the weak dinosaur bones for transport to the lab.

A New Discovery

Centuries ago, a group of men worked hard to carry a mummy case into a tomb. A pharaoh (FAIR-oh), or king of ancient <u>Egypt</u>, had just died. His name was <u>Senebkay</u>. The workers had prepared a small tomb for him. They filled it with riches.

The winds whipped the sands across the desert. Over time, sandstorms covered his tomb. People forgot his name. It would take not hundreds, but thousands of years for people to learn about this forgotten <u>Egyptian</u> pharaoh.

Egypt

Senebkay

Egyptians

Proper Noun	Reason Noun Is Capitalized
Egypt	*a country*
Senebkay	*a person*
Egyptian	*a people*
A New Discovery	*a title*

ThinkSpeakListen

Describe what happened to Senebkay's tomb.

Write to Sources

Do you think it is important to use primary sources to learn about the past? In a short essay, state your opinion and provide reasons to support it. Use evidence from two of the reading selections to support your opinion.

Type of writing

Purpose for writing

Sources you will use

Sample Essay

It is important to use primary sources because they give readers a firsthand view of past events and make them seem more real.

— The first sentence states the opinion.

One kind of primary source is "someone who has direct knowledge of the topic." For example, you can interview older family members to find out what life was like fifty years ago. They were there! And when you read a document like "The Oregon Trail" diary, you can learn about a young girl's life on a day in 1849: "Sunrise brought a magnificent sight—a herd of buffalo grazing on the plain." We can almost see what she saw!

— The body presents reasons. The reasons support the opinion of the essay. The text provides evidence to support the opinion and reasons.

Primary sources give us "firsthand knowledge" of past events and make them seem more real to us. They give us a better understanding of the past.

— The conclusion reviews the main points of your essay. It provides a closing sentence.

ThinkSpeakListen

Decide on your opinion about primary sources. Think about what you will write.

Essential Question

How do we react to changes in nature?

natural bridge

My Language Objectives

- Use nouns
- Use prepositional phrases
- Use adjectives
- Use adverbs that modify verbs
- Research and write

My Content Objectives

- Build vocabulary related to changes in nature
- Understand the processes that change nature

mountains in Alaska

rocky cliffs

143

Tornado!

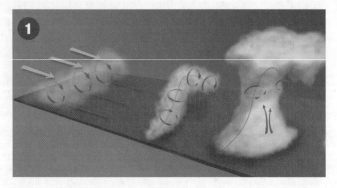

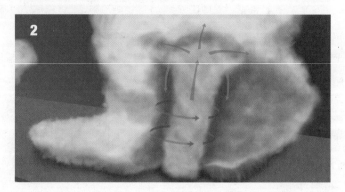

Tornadoes usually come from thunderclouds. Warm air on the ground rises to meet cooler air moving down toward Earth.

When the air masses meet, a large thundercloud forms.

As warm and cool air swirls in the thundercloud, it forms a funnel.

If the funnel is strong, it drops from the cloud and becomes a tornado!...

Some tornadoes are powerful enough to level forests and foothills.

ThinkSpeakListen

Retell key details about tornadoes.

Use Language: Nouns

Tornadoes usually come from **thunderclouds**.

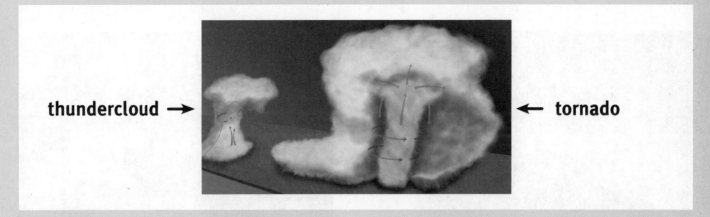

thundercloud →   ← tornado

If the **funnel** is strong, it drops from the cloud and becomes a **tornado**!

funnel →   ← thunderclouds

It spins around, forming a funnel shape, and destroys everything in its path. It tears apart buildings, uproots trees, and tosses cars as if they were toys! Although a tornado may not last very long, its damage can take years to repair.

ThinkSpeakListen

Describe how a funnel becomes a tornado.

Water's Awesome Wonder

When water moves over rock, it slowly wears away the rock. We call that *erosion*. In my opinion, erosion can create something beautiful….

The Grand Canyon began to form long ago. The Colorado River flowed across the desert floor, carving through the rock in its path.

Wind, sand, and mudslides cut away even more rock. Slowly the gash became deeper and deeper.

Today this beautiful canyon is more than a mile deep in some places. It can even be seen from space.

People visit the Grand Canyon for many reasons. It is one of the most beautiful places on Earth, with its unusually shaped rocks and colorful canyon walls.

Mule rides, hiking, and rafting down the Colorado River are three exciting ways for visitors to see the fantastic shapes and colors of the canyon.

...I think erosion and weathering created something beautiful in Arizona's desert.

The Grand Canyon is...more than just a deep hole in the ground.

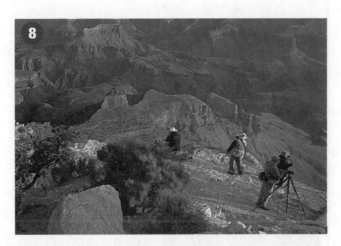

It is a sculpture that has been carved over five million years by the mighty forces of nature. And it is still being shaped today!

ThinkSpeakListen

Tell key details from "Water's Awesome Wonder."

147

The Big Blizzard

Sentence	Contraction	Word + Word
I know most children like to play in the snow, but when there's a blizzard, it's not safe.	there's it's	there + is it + is
People can't get to work, and schools are closed.	can't	can + not
With snowstorms like this, I'm ready for spring!	I'm	I + am

ThinkSpeakListen

Say a sentence using one of the contractions on this page.

Use Language: Prepositional Phrases

The Colorado River flowed <u>across</u> the desert <u>floor</u>, carving <u>through</u>
the <u>rock</u> <u>in</u> its <u>path</u>.

preposition · noun · preposition · noun preposition noun

It is one <u>of</u> the most beautiful <u>places</u> <u>on</u> <u>Earth</u>, <u>with</u> its unusually
shaped <u>rocks</u> and colorful canyon <u>walls</u>.

preposition · noun preposition noun preposition · noun · noun

It can even be seen <u>from</u> <u>space</u>.

preposition noun

Mule rides, hiking, and rafting <u>down</u> the <u>Colorado River</u> are three
exciting ways <u>for</u> <u>visitors</u> to see the fantastic shapes and colors
<u>of</u> the <u>canyon</u>.

preposition · noun · preposition noun · preposition noun

ThinkSpeakListen

Explain how the Colorado River helped form the Grand Canyon.

149

Earth's Changes by Louise Carroll

Water and wind are important elements in our daily lives.... Water and wind are also very powerful forces of nature. They shape our world....

When water wears away Earth's surfaces, it is called erosion. Strong winds also can cause erosion. Erosion changes the way Earth looks....

Earth has oceans, rivers, lakes, and streams. Most of the time these waters flow smoothly.... Ocean waves crashing against rocks can also cause erosion....

Storms can bring so much rain that rivers and lakes overflow. The water runs over the land. This is called a flood.... The land changes from the force of the moving water.

The wind can be a gentle breeze.... Wind blows against rocks and soil too. It lifts small bits and carries them elsewhere....

Wind can change the shape of a rock. It can change the shape of a sand dune. The results...can look very weird—and very beautiful!

However, wind erosion is not good for farmers' crops. Wind blows away the top layer of soil. That layer has things in it that help plants grow.

Water and wind can cause a lot of damage to Earth. They can cause damage to people's things, too....

ThinkSpeakListen

Explain some ways erosion can change Earth's surfaces.

Walls can be built around rivers that flood when it rains heavily. A wall can also keep ocean waves from striking land.

Sometimes homes are built close to shore. A wall can keep them safe from ocean water.

A wall of trees can help slow wind erosion....

Water and wind can wear away Earth's surface. They can change the way Earth looks....

Erosion and storms occur naturally. They are nature at work....

Sometimes rocks with amazing shapes are formed. Sometimes things can get damaged. Scientists are working hard to find ways to lessen the damage.

ThinkSpeakListen

Explain how people can try to prevent the effects of erosion.

Use Language: Adjectives

Water and wind are <u>important</u> <u>elements</u> in our <u>daily</u> <u>lives</u>.
                     adjective   noun   adjective noun

Over time, <u>flowing</u> <u>water</u> wears away the <u>surrounding</u> <u>rock</u> and <u>soil</u>.
           adjective   noun   adjective   noun   noun

The wind can be a <u>gentle</u> <u>breeze</u>.
                   adjective noun

Sometimes rocks with <u>amazing</u> <u>shapes</u> are formed.
                     adjective   noun

ThinkSpeakListen

Describe what wind and water can do to rocks.

My Beach

Today, I noticed something I had never seen before. It was a sign that read: BE CAREFUL! EROSION. A big piece of rock had fallen down and blocked my path. My father warned me about this. "The wind and water affect the beach every day," he said.

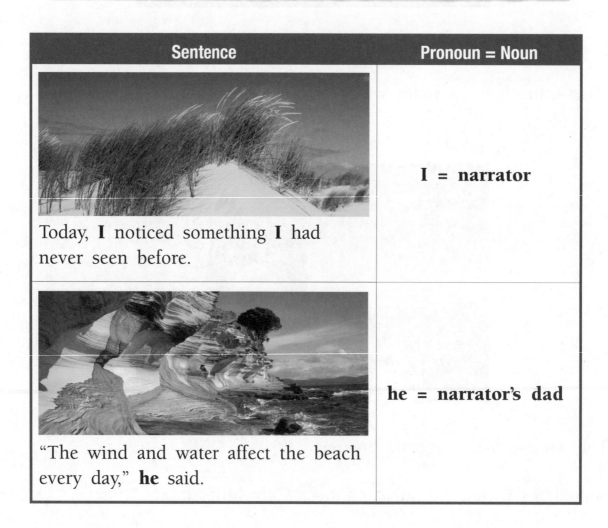

Sentence	Pronoun = Noun
Today, **I** noticed something **I** had never seen before.	**I** = narrator
"The wind and water affect the beach every day," **he** said.	**he** = narrator's dad

ThinkSpeakListen

What does the narrator's dad tell his son about erosion?

Use Language: Adverbs That Modify Verbs

Over time, flowing water wears away the
surrounding rock and soil.

verb   adverb

Most of the time these waters flow
smoothly.

verb

adverb

Scientists are working hard to find ways
to lessen the damage that water and wind
can cause.

verb   adverb

ThinkSpeakListen

What are the ways water can cause erosion?

Surf Haven Debates Its Future by Jay Forte

When Hurricane Stanley hit land last week, the small town of Surf Haven took a pounding. Stanley's powerful winds ripped up the historic boardwalk….

Town councilman Matt Fenton gave a damage report. "Forty businesses were destroyed," he said…. "We need fifty million dollars to repair all the damage."

Mayor Jan Brill said the town should rebuild the boardwalk…. "Visitors come here every summer. They spend millions of dollars. If we don't rebuild, they won't come."…

Matt Fenton agreed. "We can do this," he told the large audience at the meeting. "Remember Hurricane Nancy thirty years ago? We rebuilt then."…

5 Dr. Kay Smith from the Climate Study Group disagreed. "Ocean levels are rising.... We should turn the boardwalk into a nature preserve."...

6 Local weather expert Tom Lee agreed.... "The National Weather Panel says that in ten years, the water could rise two more inches. That means we will have even worse flooding during storms."

7 Surf Haven resident John Garcia gave other reasons for making a nature preserve.... "What people need is a beautiful sandy beach and wildlife."...

8 Shop owner Phil Pippin objected. "Easy for you to say! You don't work at the boardwalk.... I have ten employees who need a paycheck. What will they do?"...

ThinkSpeakListen
Who is telling the story? How do you know?

157

Businessman Jack Obler tried to calm the audience.... "We could have a nature preserve and shops nearby. I will help us do it."...

In my opinion, we need to listen to Mayor Brill. Surf Haven needs a new boardwalk, even if it costs fifty million dollars. —*Jim Logan, Surf Haven Resident*

We should pay attention to the scientific facts. More big storms are coming. Rebuilding the boardwalk is not a good idea. —*Jen Lund*

My opinion is that we can make the best decision if we listen to both sides of the issue. We can have a nature preserve and great new shops. —*Paula Lopez, Concerned Citizen*

ThinkSpeakListen

What choice do you think the citizens should make? Say your reasons.

Use Language: Nouns

boardwalk
compound noun

Hurricane Stanley
proper noun

visitors
plural noun

ThinkSpeakListen

Describe the kinds of damage a hurricane can cause.

Zoos: Yes or No?

Sentence	Preposition	Noun	Prepositional Phrase
Many animals live **in the wild**.	in	wild	in the wild
But some are kept **at zoos**.	at	zoos	at zoos
I've been going **to zoos** since I was three.	to	zoos	to zoos
Some animals live **in cages** instead of running free.	in	cages	in cages

ThinkSpeakListen

Make up a new sentence about the picture.

Research and Write

Choose a famous natural landmark caused by weathering and erosion. Write a short informative/ explanatory report in which you describe this landmark and explain how it was formed. Use your online research results to draft, revise, and edit your informative/explanatory report.

Type of writing

Purpose for writing

Source you will use

Sample Essay

The Badlands of South Dakota are known for their dramatic rock and clay formations, caused by millions of years of erosion.

The first paragraph states the writer's main idea.

The strange shapes found in Badlands National Park began their story 69 million years ago when an ancient sea covered the land. The sea deposited sediments. The sea went away, but rivers brought sand and soil until 28 million years ago.

The weird shapes we see now are the result of a half million years of wind and rain. The result is a landscape of colorful plateaus, pinnacles, canyons, and ravines.

The body of the report presents reasons and evidence to support the main idea.

The Badlands of South Dakota are a natural sculpture and a national treasure. The terrain is a powerful example of the extreme effects a long history of erosion can have.

The conclusion restates the main points of the report. It provides a closing sentence.

ThinkSpeakListen

Decide on the main idea you want to develop about a famous natural landmark. Research the text and discuss what you will write.

Essential Question

How do the goods we make, buy, and sell connect us?

cornfield

My Language Objectives

- Use adjectives
- Use words to link ideas
- Use nouns
- Use irregular past tense verbs
- Use signal words to tell steps in a process
- Research and write

My Content Objectives

- Build vocabulary related to producing, buying, and selling goods
- Understand how the exchange of goods shapes communities

man picking corn

woman selling corn

163

Fresh from the Market

Shoppers stroll between stands of fruits and vegetables.... A woman looks for a tomato. A man buys a box of fat, red strawberries. These people are at a farmers' market....

Farmers' markets take place... all around the world. At a farmers' market, farmers have their own stands....

...what is fresh depends on the climate....

Cherries grow best where winters aren't too cold and summers aren't too hot....

Today, it doesn't matter where people live. People can still get the foods they want. But they can get the freshest food at a farmers' market.

ThinkSpeakListen

Talk about why you can get the freshest food at a farmers' market.

Use Language: Adjectives

A man buys a box of <u>fat, red</u> <u>strawberries</u>.
adjective adjective   noun

At a <u>farmers' market</u>, farmers have their own stands.
adjective   noun

Cherries grow best where <u>winters</u> aren't too <u>cold</u>
and <u>summers</u> aren't too <u>hot</u>.
noun   adjective
noun   adjective

But they can get the <u>freshest</u> <u>food</u> at a <u>farmers' market</u>.
adjective   noun   adjective   noun

ThinkSpeakListen

Say a sentence with a noun and an adjective.

165

Goat and Bear in Business

Goat and Bear were best friends. One day, the two decided to go into business so they could earn some money. "I'm going to sell my delicious baked potatoes!" said Bear. "I'll sell my delectable raisin buns!" exclaimed Goat....

...they waited for the customers to arrive. Before long, Goat was hungry. He had a nickel in his pocket, so he purchased one of Bear's potatoes.

166

Soon Bear was hungry, too. So he took the nickel he had made and bought one of Goat's raisin buns. Goat was delighted with his first sale! Now he had a nickel. To celebrate, he purchased another potato from Bear....

...Goat and Bear went back and forth in the same way.... However, when they counted their money... They didn't understand how they could...have only one nickel!

Think Speak Listen

Tell what happens first, next, and last in the story.

A Baker's Dozen

Long ago, there lived a fine baker.... As he stood in his shop, he felt happy....

Suddenly, a woman with a pointy hat and beady eyes marched in. "I want a dozen rolls," she demanded. The baker counted out twelve rolls and wrapped them carefully. "Other bakers give me thirteen rolls," she growled.

"A dozen means twelve," he answered.

"I want a <u>dozen</u> <u>rolls</u>."

    adjective   noun

"Other bakers give me <u>thirteen</u> <u>rolls</u>."

            adjective   noun

ThinkSpeakListen

Find one more sentence from "A Baker's Dozen" with a number adjective.

168

Use Language: Words That Link Ideas

Fresh from the Market

Idea	Linking Word	Idea
People get the freshest fruits	**and**	vegetables from nearby farms.

Goat and Bear in Business

Idea	Linking Word	Idea
He had a nickel in his pocket,	**so**	he purchased one of Bear's potatoes.
So he took the nickel he had made	**and**	bought one of Goat's raisin buns.

ThinkSpeakListen

Tell the ideas linked by the word "and."

From Pine Tree to Pizza Box

by Amy and Richard Hutchings

Trees are very important natural resources.... Trees provide homes for animals, including insects, birds, and squirrels....

People also use the wood from some trees to make many things.... Pine trees are good trees for making paper and cardboard products....

First, trees are cut down. Then they are chopped into logs.... Logs are made into planks, boards, and other pieces, or chips, of wood. Wood chips are used to make cardboard.

Next, the wood chips become a pulp.... It gets pressed into thin rolls of strong paper.

Three layers of paper at a time are then fed into a machine....

5

The cardboard can be cut, shaped, and printed on. It can then be folded into different types of finished products....

6

Can you think of some things you can buy in a cardboard box? Cereal, sneakers, and games are packaged in cardboard boxes. So is pizza!

7

Cardboard is also used to ship things.... When people move, they use a lot of cardboard boxes to pack their things....

8

It is important to recycle cardboard and other paper products.... When cardboard is recycled, fewer trees need to be cut down.

ThinkSpeakListen

Explain why recycling is good for both forests and businesses.

How does something get recycled? It begins with you! You and your family put your clean used cardboard into a recycling bin.

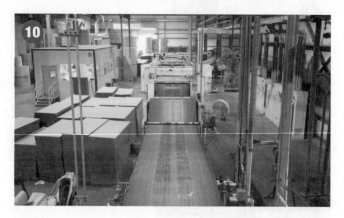

The bin gets taken to a recycling center. At the recycling center, everything is sorted.... Some things cannot be used again...

The cardboard that can be used again is sent to a special factory. This factory turns the old cardboard into like-new cardboard....

Trees are important natural resources.... Recycling paper products, including cardboard, is one way to help make sure we will always have big, beautiful trees!

ThinkSpeakListen

Tell one thing about how cardboard is used.

Use Language: Nouns

tree

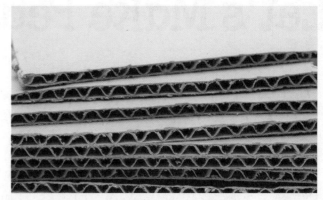

cardboard

bin

animals

logs

box

ThinkSpeakListen

Use nouns to name products that come from trees.

Let's Make Peanut Butter

At the factory, the peanut shells are quickly taken off by a machine. Next, the peanuts are roasted in ovens and the skins are taken off. Other machines grind the peanuts into peanut butter. Then the peanut butter is poured into jars. Finally, the jars are sold to stores.

<u>Next</u>, the peanuts are roasted in ovens…
signal word

<u>Then</u> the peanut butter is poured into jars.
signal word

<u>Finally</u>, the jars are sold to stores.
signal word

ThinkSpeakListen

Say a sentence using signal words to describe the steps in making a peanut butter sandwich.

174

Use Language: Irregular Past Tense Verbs

Sentence	Present Tense Verb	Irregular Past Tense Verb
Some trees **grow** nuts or fruits…	**grow**	**grew**
People also use the wood from some trees to **make** many things.	**make**	**made**
It **is** good for making boxes.	**is**	**was**
Next, the wood chips **become** a pulp.	**become**	**became**
Can you think of some things you can **buy** in a cardboard box?	**buy**	**bought**

ThinkSpeakListen

Describe a time when you or a family member bought something that came in a cardboard box.

175

The Paper Dinosaurs by Janine Scott

Mrs. Adams said, "Let's make new things from old newspapers. Then, we can sell what we make at the school fair. That will help pay for a trip to the Science Museum. Who has an idea?"…

…Amy said, "Let's make paper dinosaurs."…

First, they tore some newspapers into strips. Next, they rolled other pieces into balls…. Before long, a dinosaur took shape.

"It's your turn now," Mrs. Adams told the class. "Look at the dinosaur books in the library. Choose your favorite dinosaur to make."…

The moon shone on the paper dinosaurs. A purple light glowed and the dinosaurs twitched. The movement was so tiny that if you had blinked, you would have missed it….

176

The dinosaurs stumbled about in the dark.... Then, accidentally, one stepped on a computer mouse. Suddenly, dinosaurs a hundred times bigger than the paper dinosaurs charged toward them!...

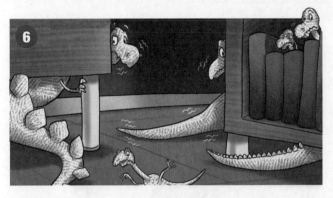

"Run for your lives!" cried the biggest paper dinosaur....

The smallest paper dinosaur stepped in some leftover glue and paper. She was so scared she didn't feel the squishy, slushy paper beneath her foot....

"Look," cried Amy as she walked into class. "Our dinosaurs have set."...

As Amy reached for the paint, she saw a small dinosaur footprint in some newspaper....

"Mrs. Adams," she cried. "I know another thing we could make with old newspapers."...

"Dinosaur footprint fossils!" yelled Amy.

ThinkSpeakListen

Tell how Amy gets the idea to make dinosaur footprint fossils.

"Great idea!" said Toby. "We could have a Dinosaur Dig at the fair. People could pay to dig for fossils buried in sand."

The class bubbled over with excitement... The children made footprint fossils in the mushy newspaper....

The Dinosaur Dig was a huge success....

...the children were most impressed with one of the littlest dinosaur displays. It was a fossil of a tiny dinosaur's footprint.

In fact, Amy thought it looked exactly like the footprint she had found. Of course, that wouldn't be possible—or would it?

ThinkSpeakListen

Why are the children more interested in the tiny dinosaur footprint than in the actual dinosaur skeletons?

Use Language: Signal Words That Tell Steps in a Process

<u>First</u>, they tore some newspapers into strips. <u>Next</u>, they rolled other
signal word   signal word
pieces into balls.

<u>Then</u>, she dipped the paper strips into glue and placed them around
signal word
the balls.

<u>Later</u> that night, Earth's shadow fell on a blue moon.
signal word

ThinkSpeakListen
Say another word that signals the end of a series of steps in a
process.

Our Class Knows!

Mr. Knight's class has a big problem. The students need to raise money for a field trip. "You can't sell food," said Mr. Knight. "You can't sell T-shirts, either. It's against school rules."

"What can we sell, then?" asked the class.

"I know," said Jack. "We can sell knowledge!"

"What?" asked the class.

"We will sell advice," said Jack. "We will answer any question asked. No question is too dumb. No answer too hard to find. We will never be wrong!"

"Fun!" said the class. They started making signs.

"I'll write the price for our advice on my sign," said Dan.

"I'll write, 'My advice is the best!'" said Marta.

ThinkSpeakListen

Go through a book or magazine and say the proper nouns you see.

Research and Write

You learned about goods that people make, buy, and sell. Choose a good that your class can make and sell. Write a short story in which you describe a good and how your class would make and sell it.

Type of writing
Purpose for writing

Sample Essay

Our class needed art supplies—badly. We wanted to make something to sell at the Art Fair downtown, but how could we do it without supplies?

The first sentences set up a conflict: What needs to be done?

Marcel had an idea. He brought it to Mr. Kim, our teacher. "We don't have much, but we have plenty of glue. Water's free. So are old newspapers."

Mr. Kim smiled. "So what should we make?"

The body shows the characters dealing with the problem, or conflict.

That weekend our papier-mâché zoo was a hit! We sold giraffes, cheetahs, elephants, and lions. All that old paper and glue turned into paper pads, brushes, and paint in every color of the rainbow.

The end of the story shows the conflict being resolved.

ThinkSpeakListen

Decide on your story's conflict. Discuss how that conflict might be resolved.

Essential Question

How can something old become new?

liquid

My Language Objectives

- Use conjunctions
- Use serial commas
- Use "and" to link verbs
- Use multiple-meaning words
- Use past tense verbs
- Research and write

My Content Objectives

- Build vocabulary related to states of matter
- Understand how matter changes from one state to another

solid

gas

183

The Art of Origami

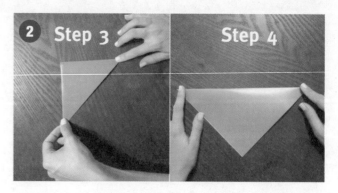

1: Begin with a square piece of white or colored paper....

2: Fold the paper in half from top corner to bottom corner. Now you have a triangle.

3: Fold the triangle in half again, by folding the left point to the right point.

4: Unfold the triangle. There will be a crease down the middle.

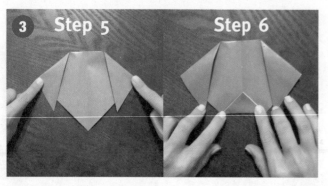

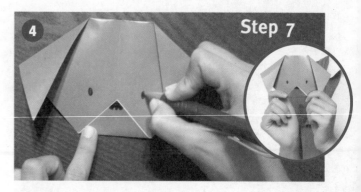

5: To make the ears, fold both corners of the triangle down...

6: Fold back the point at the bottom of the dog's head.

7: Draw two eyes and a nose. Now your dog has a face....

How amazing is that!

ThinkSpeakListen

Talk about what might happen if any of these steps were left out.

Use Language: Conjunctions

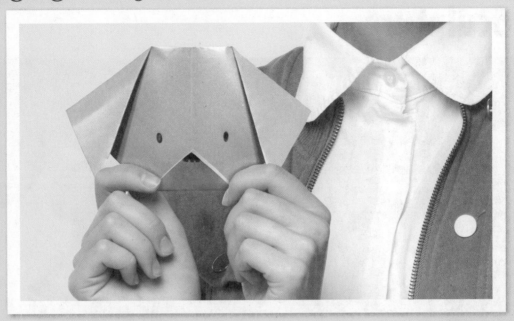

Idea	Conjunction	Idea
The directions are easy to follow,	**so**	let's get started.
Begin with a square piece of white	**or**	colored paper.
Fold the triangle in half again,	**by**	folding the left point to the right point.
You began with a square piece of paper	**and**	transformed it into a dog's face.

ThinkSpeakListen
Use a conjunction to connect two ideas in a sentence.

185

Sand Sculpture

Picture yourself at the beach on a hot summer day—soft sand, crashing waves, squawking seagulls, and sunny skies. Did you remember to bring some pails and shovels? If so, you have everything you need to build a sand castle....

For some people, sand castles are more than just fun at the beach.... Sand sculptors enter competitions to win big prizes. When they compete, they use the same simple items as you do—shovels, molds, sand, and water.

But their knowledge of science, construction, and art results in some amazing creations....

...water creates tiny "bridges" that hold the grains of sand together. Sand sculptors know just how much water to add....

The sculptors work quickly to stack their blocks of hard, wet sand.... They carve every detail with fine tools. Finally, a stunning work of art appears—for a little while, anyway.

ThinkSpeakListen

Take turns and tell what happens first, next, and last in the story.

World's Best Glass Art

How does Dale <u>make</u> his art? He is an expert at
_{verb}

<u>blowing</u> glass. First he <u>heats</u> sand and a few other
_{verb}   _{verb}

materials. After that, he <u>blows</u> into the hot, liquid
_{verb}

mixture to <u>shape</u> the glass. It <u>takes</u> a long time to
_{verb}   _{verb}

<u>make</u> one small bowl. It can <u>take</u> months to <u>make</u>
_{verb}   _{verb}   _{verb}

one of Dale's bigger art pieces. Dale's talent has

<u>amazed</u> people all over the world.
_{verb}

ThinkSpeakListen
Say a sentence that describes an action.

Use Language: Serial Commas

Picture yourself at the beach on a hot summer day—soft sand, crashing waves, squawking seagulls, and sunny skies.

serial commas

serial commas

When they compete, they use the same simple items as you do—shovels, molds, sand, and water.

serial commas

But their knowledge of science, construction, and art results in some amazing creations.

serial commas

ThinkSpeakListen
Consider the steps sculptors go through in building a sand castle. Then create a sentence that lists those steps using serial commas.

Changing Matter by Jay Brewster

Everything in the world is made of matter. There are three kinds of matter: solid, liquid, and gas....

...one kind of matter can sometimes change into another ...

Hold up a glass that has liquid in it. You are holding all three kinds of matter! The glass itself is an example of solid matter. The drink is an example of liquid matter.... Air is a mixture of gases...

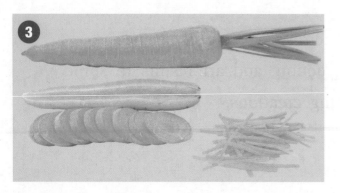

You can change the size of matter.... A carrot is a solid piece of matter. You can change the size of the carrot by asking an adult to help you cut it into several small pieces or by shredding it.

You can change the size of a liquid, too. Take a glass with water and pour half into another glass.... You have changed the size of the liquid by dividing it.

Shape is another property of matter that can be changed.... Get a bowl and pour the water into the bowl. By transferring the water from one container to another, you have changed its shape.

Gas can change its shape, too.... Put a straw into a glass of milk and blow air into the straw. You will see bubbles moving around... Those bubbles are filled with air.

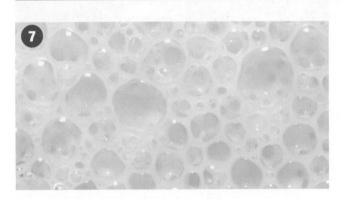

Remember, air is a mixture of gases. By blowing into the milk, you made the gases in the glass move and change shape.

When matter undergoes a severe change in temperature, it can change from one state of matter into another.

ThinkSpeakListen

How might weather affect states of water?

Water can exist in all three states of matter. When water is very cold, it freezes… Frozen water, or ice, is solid matter that can have different shapes.…

For ice to change from a solid back into a liquid, it needs to be heated up. The ice will melt, and it will be flowing water again.…

…when water in a pot on the stove starts to boil, it starts to bubble. Steam starts to rise… Steam is liquid water that has turned into a gas.

There are three different kinds of matter that make up our world.… Some matter can even change from one kind of matter into another.

ThinkSpeakListen

Tell how water might change from one state of matter to another as it travels from a cold mountain top to a steamy hot spring.

Use Language: Link Verbs with "And"

solid   liquid   gas

Take a glass with water and pour half into another glass.
verb   link verb

Get a bowl and pour the water into the bowl.
verb   link verb

Air is a mixture of gases and is therefore an example of gas matter.
verb   link verb

When water is very cold, it freezes and becomes ice.
verb   link   verb

ThinkSpeakListen

Make up a sentence with two verbs. Link the verbs with "and."

Sand Becomes Glass!

The man kept heating, cooling, and then reheating the mixture. It was unsafe for us to get too close.

<u>At first</u>, the mixture was orange-red. You could pour
linking phrase

it like milk. <u>Then</u> he took some and blew into it
linking word

using a long tube called a blowpipe. <u>As it cooled</u>, he
linking phrase

shaped and reshaped the glass until it was the correct size. Oh, how fun it was! I want to return some day.

ThinkSpeakListen

Describe what the glassblower does with the mixture.

194

Use Language: Multiple-Meaning Words

Sentence	Meaning	Possible Other Meaning
Some properties **can** change.	able to	a metal container
For ice to change from a solid **back** into a liquid, it needs to be heated up.	return	the opposite of front
A **kind** of matter is also called a state of matter.	type	nice
Shape is another **property** of matter that can be changed.	quality	possession, piece of land
You can **change** some properties of matter.	alter	coins

ThinkSpeakListen
Say a sentence that shows the other meaning of one of the words above.

How Mount Rushmore Was Made by Kira Freed

Imagine that you're a sculptor… Will you use clay, stone, metal, or wood? An artist named Gutzon Borglum used a mountain!

Mount Rushmore is the art that Borglum created.…

This sculpture is on a rock cliff in South Dakota. Borglum carved the presidents' faces very large so people could see them from far away. Each face is sixty feet tall—as tall as a six-story building!…

Borglum went to South Dakota in 1924.… When he saw Mount Rushmore, he knew it was the perfect place for his art. The mountain was tall enough to see from far away.…

He wanted the world to know about some great Americans. He wanted to honor "American achievement." He decided to carve four presidents on the mountain.

Borglum started by making drawings of the presidents. Then he used the drawings to make plaster models. After Borglum finished the models, he was ready to start carving....

The people of South Dakota liked the idea of the project.... Over time, they arranged for the United States to pay for most of the work....

Workers had to climb hundreds of stairs each day.... They used heavy drills to make holes in the rock. They put dynamite into the holes to blast away the outer rock....

After the outer rock was gone, workers were close to the rock surface that would remain.... Then Borglum himself worked on the rock. His artistry made the presidents look more alive.

ThinkSpeakListen

Find and say aloud a verb on the page that tells what Borglum and his workers did to the rock.

Nearly 400 men and women worked on Mount Rushmore. The workers were not artists—many were ranchers, miners, or lumbermen.... The work was difficult, and the days were long....

Washington's head was finished in 1930. Jefferson's was completed in 1936, and Lincoln's in 1937. Finally, in 1939, Roosevelt's head was done....

The Mount Rushmore sculpture took fourteen years to complete. Work began in 1927 and ended in 1941....

More than fifty million people have seen it since...1930.... They come to honor four presidents... They also come to view an amazing sculpture.

ThinkSpeakListen

Summarize in a few sentences what Borglum did to create Mount Rushmore.

Use Language: Past Tense Verbs

Sentence	Present Tense Verb	Past Tense Verb
Mount Rushmore is the art that Borglum **created**.	create	creat**ed**
Borglum **carved** the presidents' faces very large.	carve	carv**ed**
The rock **looked** strong enough to carve.	look	look**ed**
Workers **removed** almost half a million tons of rock.	remove	remov**ed**

ThinkSpeakListen

Say another sentence about Mount Rushmore using a past tense verb.

Beautiful Ice Cities

Each year in China, there is a big winter festival. They make a city out of ice and snow. The clear, smooth surfaces of the buildings are nothing but frozen water. There are also snow slides, snow mazes, and even snow dinosaurs. Although ice is colorless, the city is beautiful!

<u>snow</u> <u>slides</u>
adjective noun

<u>big</u> <u>winter</u> <u>festival</u>
adjective adjective noun

ThinkSpeakListen

Say a sentence about the town or city where you live. Use adjectives to describe it.

Research and Write

In this unit, you learned about how people can change the size, shape, and states of matter to make things. Which property of matter do you think is most important? Why? In a short essay, state your opinion and provide one or more reasons to support it.

Use your research results to draft, revise, and edit your short essay.

Type of writing

Purpose for writing

Reasons

Source you will use

Sample Essay

The most important thing about matter is that it can keep its shape.

> **The first sentence states the opinion.**

It's true that matter can come in forms that aren't solid at all. For example, "The ice will melt, and it will be flowing water again," one article says. It can also become steam, a kind of gas. But the kinds of matter that stay solid let us build things. Because matter can be solid, we can have buildings to work and study in. We can have bridges and roads to get around on.

> **The body presents reasons. The reasons support the opinion of the essay. The text provides evidence to support the opinion and reasons.**

Solid matter lets us build things that last. People can use some of these things every day to live and work. There are also wonderful creations, like Mount Rushmore, that we can always admire.

> **The conclusion reviews the main points of your essay. It provides a closing sentence.**

ThinkSpeakListen

Decide on your opinion about matter. Then research the texts in this unit and discuss what you will write.

Common Core State Standards

	CA CCSS **Reading Standards for Literature**
RL.2.1	Ask and answer such questions as *who, what, where, when, why,* and *how* to demonstrate understanding of key details in a text.
RL.2.2	Recount stories, including fables and folktales from diverse cultures, and determine their central message, lesson, or moral.
RL.2.3	Describe how characters in a story respond to major events and challenges.
RL.2.4	Describe how words and phrases (e.g., regular beats, alliteration, rhymes, repeated lines) supply rhythm and meaning in a story, poem, or song. **(See grade 2 Language standards 4–6 for additional expectations.) CA**
RL.2.5	Describe the overall structure of a story, including describing how the beginning introduces the story and the ending concludes the action.
RL.2.6	Acknowledge differences in the points of view of characters, including by speaking in a different voice for each character when reading dialogue aloud.
RL.2.7	Use information gained from the illustrations and words in a print or digital text to demonstrate understanding of its characters, setting, or plot.
RL.2.9	Compare and contrast two or more versions of the same story (e.g., Cinderella stories) by different authors or from different cultures.
RL.2.10	By the end of the year, read and comprehend literature, including stories and poetry, in the grades 2–3 text complexity band proficiently, with scaffolding as needed at the high end of the range.

	CA CCSS **Reading Standards for Informational Text**
RI.2.1	Ask and answer such questions as *who, what, where, when, why,* and *how* to demonstrate understanding of key details in a text.
RI.2.2	Identify the main topic of a multiparagraph text as well as the focus of specific paragraphs within the text.
RI.2.3	Describe the connection between a series of historical events, scientific ideas or concepts, or steps in technical procedures in a text.
RI.2.4	Determine the meaning of words and phrases in a text relevant to a grade 2 topic or subject area. **(See grade 2 Language standards 4–6 for additional expectations.) CA**
RI.2.5	Know and use various text features (e.g., captions, bold print, subheadings, glossaries, indexes, electronic menus, icons) to locate key facts or information in a text efficiently.
RI.2.6	Identify the main purpose of a text, including what the author wants to answer, explain, or describe.
RI.2.7	Explain how specific images (e.g., a diagram showing how a machine works) contribute to and clarify a text.
RI.2.8	Describe how reasons support specific points the author makes in a text.
RI.2.9	Compare and contrast the most important points presented by two texts on the same topic.
RI.2.10	By the end of year, read and comprehend informational texts, including history/social studies, science, and technical texts, in the grades 2–3 text complexity band proficiently, with scaffolding as needed at the high end of the range.

CA CCSS Reading Standards for Foundational Skills

RF.2.3	Know and apply grade-level phonics and word analysis skills in decoding words **both in isolation and in text. CA** a. Distinguish long and short vowels when reading regularly spelled one-syllable words. b. Know spelling-sound correspondences for additional common vowel teams. c. Decode regularly spelled two-syllable words with long vowels. d. Decode words with common prefixes and suffixes. e. Identify words with inconsistent but common spelling-sound correspondences. f. Recognize and read grade-appropriate irregularly spelled words.
RF.2.4	4. Read with sufficient accuracy and fluency to support comprehension. a. Read on-level text with purpose and understanding. b. Read on-level text orally with accuracy, appropriate rate, and expression on successive readings. c. Use context to confirm or self-correct word recognition and understanding, rereading as necessary.

CA CCSS Writing Standards

W.2.1	Write opinion pieces in which they introduce the topic or book they are writing about, state an opinion, supply reasons that support the opinion, use linking words (e.g., *because, and, also*) to connect opinion and reasons, and provide a concluding statement or section.
W.2.2	Write informative/explanatory texts in which they introduce a topic, use facts and definitions to develop points, and provide a concluding statement or section.
W.2.3	Write narratives in which they recount a well-elaborated event or short sequence of events, include details to describe actions, thoughts, and feelings, use temporal words to signal event order, and provide a sense of closure.
W.2.4	**With guidance and support from adults, produce writing in which the development and organization are appropriate to task and purpose. (Grade-specific expectations for writing types are defined in standards 1–3 above.) CA**
W.2.5	With guidance and support from adults and peers, focus on a topic and strengthen writing as needed by revising and editing.
W.2.6	With guidance and support from adults, use a variety of digital tools to produce and publish writing, including in collaboration with peers.
W.2.7	Participate in shared research and writing projects (e.g., read a number of books on a single topic to produce a report; record science observations).
W.2.8	Recall information from experiences or gather information from provided sources to answer a question.
W.2.10	**Write routinely over extended time frames (time for research, reflection, and revision) and shorter time frames (a single sitting or a day or two) for a range of discipline-specific tasks, purposes, and audiences. CA**

CA CCSS Speaking and Listening Standards

SL.2.1	Participate in collaborative conversations with diverse partners about *grade 2 topics and texts* with peers and adults in small and larger groups. a. Follow agreed-upon rules for discussions (e.g., gaining the floor in respectful ways, listening to others with care, speaking one at a time about the topics and texts under discussion). b. Build on others' talk in conversations by linking their comments to the remarks of others. c. Ask for clarification and further explanation as needed about the topics and texts under discussion.
SL.2.2	Recount or describe key ideas or details from a text read aloud or information presented orally or through other media. **a. Give and follow three- and four-step oral directions. CA**
SL.2.3	Ask and answer questions about what a speaker says in order to clarify comprehension, gather additional information, or deepen understanding of a topic or issue.
SL.2.4	Tell a story or recount an experience with appropriate facts and relevant, descriptive details, speaking audibly in coherent sentences. **a. Plan and deliver a narrative presentation that: recounts a well-elaborated event, includes details, reflects a logical sequence, and provides a conclusion. CA**
SL.2.5	Create audio recordings of stories or poems; add drawings or other visual displays to stories or recounts of experiences when appropriate to clarify ideas, thoughts, and feelings.
SL.2.6	Produce complete sentences when appropriate to task and situation in order to provide requested detail or clarification. (See grade 2 Language standards 1 and 3 for specific expectations.)

CA CCSS Language Standards

L.2.1	Demonstrate command of the conventions of standard English grammar and usage when writing or speaking. a. Use collective nouns (e.g., *group*). b. Form and use frequently occurring irregular plural nouns (e.g., *feet, children, teeth, mice, fish*). c. Use reflexive pronouns (e.g., *myself, ourselves*). d. Form and use the past tense of frequently occurring irregular verbs (e.g., *sat, hid, told*). e. Use adjectives and adverbs, and choose between them depending on what is to be modified. f. Produce, expand, and rearrange complete simple and compound sentences (e.g., *The boy watched the movie; The little boy watched the movie; The action movie was watched by the little boy*). g. **Create readable documents with legible print. CA**
L.2.2	2. Demonstrate command of the conventions of standard English capitalization, punctuation, and spelling when writing. a. Capitalize dates and names of people. b. Use end punctuation for sentences. c. Use commas in dates and to separate single words in a series. d. Use conventional spelling for words with common spelling patterns and for frequently occurring irregular words. e. Spell untaught words phonetically, drawing on phonemic awareness and spelling conventions.
L.2.3	Use knowledge of language and its conventions when writing, speaking, reading, or listening. a. Compare formal and informal uses of English.
L.2.4	Determine or clarify the meaning of unknown and multiple-meaning words and phrases based on *grade 2 reading and content*, choosing flexibly from an array of strategies. a. Use sentence-level context as a clue to the meaning of a word or phrase. b. Determine the meaning of the new word formed when a known prefix is added to a known word (e.g., *happy/unhappy, tell/retell*). c. Use a known root word as a clue to the meaning of an unknown word with the same root (e.g., *addition, additional*). d. Use knowledge of the meaning of individual words to predict the meaning of compound words (e.g., *birdhouse, lighthouse, housefly; bookshelf, notebook, bookmark*). e. Use glossaries and beginning dictionaries, both print and digital, to determine or clarify the meaning of words and phrases **in all content areas. CA**
L.2.5	Demonstrate understanding of word relationships and nuances in word meanings. a. Identify real-life connections between words and their use (e.g., describe foods that are *spicy* or *juicy*). b. Distinguish shades of meaning among closely related verbs (e.g., *toss, throw, hurl*) and closely related adjectives (e.g., *thin, slender, skinny, scrawny*).
L.2.6	Use words and phrases acquired through conversations, reading and being read to, and responding to texts, including using adjectives and adverbs to describe (e.g., *When other kids are happy that makes me happy*).

California English Language Development Standards

CA ELD Part I: Interacting in Meaningful Ways

ELD.PI.2.1	Exchanging information and ideas with others through oral collaborative conversations on a range of social and academic topics
ELD.PI.2.2	Interacting with others in written English in various communicative forms (print, communicative technology, and multimedia)
ELD.PI.2.3	Offering and supporting opinions and negotiating with others in communicative exchanges
ELD.PI.2.4	Adapting language choices to various contexts (based on task, purpose, audience, and text type)
ELD.PI.2.5	Listening actively to spoken English in a range of social and academic contexts
ELD.PI.2.6	Reading closely literary and informational texts and viewing multimedia to determine how meaning is conveyed explicitly and implicitly through language
ELD.PI.2.7	Evaluating how well writers and speakers use language to support ideas and opinions with details or reasons depending on modality, text type, purpose, audience, topic, and content area
ELD.PI.2.8	Analyzing how writers and speakers use vocabulary and other language resources for specific purposes (to explain, persuade, entertain, etc.) depending on modality, text type, purpose, audience, topic, and content area
ELD.PI.2.9	Expressing information and ideas in formal oral presentations on academic topics
ELD.PI.2.10	Writing literary and informational texts to present, describe, and explain ideas and information, using appropriate technology
ELD.PI.2.11	Supporting own opinions and evaluating others' opinions in speaking and writing
ELD.PI.2.12	Selecting and applying varied and precise vocabulary and language structures to effectively convey ideas

CA ELD Part II: Learning About How English Works

ELD.PII.2.1	Understanding text structure
ELD.PII.2.2	Understanding cohesion
ELD.PII.2.3	Using verbs and verb phrases
ELD.PII.2.4	Using nouns and noun phrases
ELD.PII.2.5	Modifying to add details
ELD.PII.2.6	Connecting ideas
ELD.PII.2.7	Condensing ideas

CA ELD Part III: Using Foundational Literacy Skills

ELD.PIII.2.1	See Appendix A [in *Foundational Literacy Skills for English Learners*] for information on teaching reading foundational skills to English learners of various profiles based on age, native language, native language writing system, schooling experience, and literacy experience and proficiency. Some considerations are: • Native language and literacy (e.g., phoneme awareness or print concept skills in native language) should be assessed for potential transference to English language and literacy. • Similarities between native language and English should be highlighted (e.g., phonemes or letters that are the same in both languages). • Differences between native language and English should be highlighted (e.g., some phonemes in English may not exist in the student's native language; native language syntax may be different from English syntax).

Benchmark ADVANCE

Texts *for* English Language Development

Credits
Editor: Joanne Tangorra
Creative Director: Laurie Berger
Art Director: Doug McGredy
Production: Kosta Triantafillis
Director of Photography: Doug Schneider
Photo Assistant: Jackie Friedman

Photo credits: Page 3a: © John Snowdon / Alamy; Page 4b, 5a: J. BAYLOR ROBERTS/National Geographic Creative; Page 4c, 5c: © United Archives GmbH / Alamy; Page 4d: © Don Despain / Alamy; Page 5e: © Dan Lamont/CORBIS; Page 10a: © Ron Sachs/Corbis; Page 10d: ASSOCIATED PRESS; Page 12c, 12d: © David R. Frazier Photolibrary, Inc. / Alamy; Page 13c: © Image Source Plus / Alamy; Page 44c: NaturePL; Page 44d, 45a: Minden Pictures; Page 44e: © Stefan Christmann/Corbis; Page 60a: © Gregg Vignal / Alamy; Page 60b: © Images-USA / Alamy; Page 60c: © shapencolour / Alamy; Page 84a,89a: ClassicStock.com; Page 84b, 85a, 89f; Page © Wolff & Tritschler/Corbis; Page 84d: Birmingham History Center; Page 86a,89c; Page: © Scott Camazine / Alamy; Page 86c, 89e: NaturePL;Page 90b, 90d: Library of Congress; Page 87b, 96a, 96b, 96c, 96d, 97b, 97a,98b, 98d: ASSOCIATED PRESS; Page 90f, 92d, 91a, 91c, 91d, 92b, 92c, 92f, 95: Granger, NYC; Page 92k: © Underwood & Underwood/Corbis; Page 92m: © John Henshall / Alamy; Page 97d, 98a, 98c: AMELIE-BENOIST / BSIP/Newscom; Page 123a: © age fotostock / Alamy; Page 124c, 130g, 132k, 132f, 132g: Granger, NYC; Page 124e, 129c: © National Geographic Image Collection / Alamy; Page 126a: © Corbis; Page 127a: © FLPA / Alamy; Page 129a: © Jim Nicholson / Alamy; Page 129b: © Robert HENNO / Alamy; 129c: © National Geographic Image Collection / Alamy; Page 130d, 131a: Rue des Archives / Granger NYC;, Page 130h: Library of Congress; Page 132a, 132b: HIP / Art Resource, NY; Page 133d: © Julie Lemberger/Corbis; Page 136d, 136e, 137c,138b, 137d, 138a: Black Hills Institute of Geological Research, Inc.; Page 144a, 144b, 145a: Monica Schroeder / Science Source; Page 152a: Stephen Morton / Stringer; Page 153a: Michael Busselle; Page 156b: Worldwide/Newscom; 156d J.W.Alker imageBROKER/Newscom; Page 144b, 144c, 144d, 144e, 144f, 144g, 144h: Lizette Nieto; Page 147a, 149b: © Gunter Marx Photography/CORBIS; Page 147b, 149c: alexvirid/shutterstock.com; Page 148: © Mika/Corbis; Page 151a, 153e: Doug Schneider; Page 156d: © Bettmann/CORBIS; Page 157a, 158b, 157d, 159b: Library of Congress; Page 158c. © Mike Theiss/National Geographic Society/Corbis; Page 160a: © Stephen Shaver/ZUMA Press/ Corbis; Page 160b: © Zhu Zhenghua /Xinhua Press/Corbis

ISBN: 978-1-5021-6644-9 (hardcover)
ISBN: BE2775 (paperback)